One Month in Politics

The Diary of a Candid Candidate

Crispian Besley

Dedication

For all those who helped me in my campaign and especially for each one of the 8,468 constituents in Kettering who put their trust in me and voted for Reform.

Acknowledgements

Juliet Eckersley, Justin Besley, Richard Frankel, Stuart Beaty, Jack Beaty, Ben Habib, Simon Besley, Sean Lever, Gawain Towler, Charles Cook, Richard Tice, Adam Richardson, Roz Lloyd-Williams, Nick and Georgia Matterson, Tony Owens, Antony Antoniou, Eddie McDonald, Paul Hogan, Scott Cameron, Sam Wildman, Pam Austin, Ian Blackwell, Carole Shrigley, Daniel Howes, Janice Howes, Stan Taylor, Fred Rainbow, David Biddle, Sandra Biddle, Liz Sharman, James Squire, Janet Squire, Tony Webster, Tony Green, Steve Walsh, Alan Currall, Ian Bloomfield, Ray Kemp, Ian Preston-Kleine, John Marshall, Andrew Buckley, Maria Thomson, Angela Hawkes, Glenis Cassidy, Francis Leadbetter, Linda Leadbetter, Ian Ashton, Ivan Humphrey, Martyn Ayre, Mike Cross, Brian Benneyworth, David Johnson, Martin Bradshaw, Ashley Lawman, Steve Walsh, Dave Johnson, Mark Warren, Terry Hewison, Tricia Jones, Brenda Baverstock, Mike Wilford, Janet Diaz-Santana, Randall Foster, Steve Male, Kevin Sills, David Hutchinson?, Paula Swift, Ray Kemp, Colin Free, Andrew Robinson, Michael Wilford, Simon Turner, Lisa and Mark Warren, Jamie McAllinden, Paula Swift, Mike Wilford, Steve Fuller, Tim Fallon, Christine Manning.

About the Author

Crispian Besley is a former investment banker, racing driver, Parliamentary Candidate and award-winning author.

He had never previously held any aspirations to be a politician-let alone an MP but stood as a Parliamentary Candidate in the 2024 General Election and had enough credibility to win almost 17% of the vote in a constituency he had barely set foot in before. This was achieved during a very short campaign lasting only a few weeks.

Also published by the author

Driven to Crime: True Stories of Chicanery in Motorsport

ISBN: 978-1-910505-70-0

Published: October 2022

www.evropublishing.com

INTRODUCTION

After the snap General Election was called by Prime Minister Rishi Sunak on 22nd May 2024, with just six weeks' notice, Reform UK-the newest but fastest-growing party in British politics-was more wrong-footed than the opposition. With limited resources and only minimal infrastructure, the party faced a mad scramble to field as many Parliamentary Candidates (PCs) as possible in the 650 constituency seats available.

In a magnificent result, the party won five seats and finished second in 98 constituencies, 89 of those behind Labour.

Known to the party's co-founder, Richard Tice, Crispian Besley was 'parachuted' at the last moment into a local constituency in his home county of Northamptonshire. Although it wasn't exactly a comfortable 'landing', the experience gave him the opportunity of a lifetime, one that would not have been afforded by the mainstream parties, and was so last-minute that he had even less warning than others due to the PM's late decision to call the election.

Presented in diary form, interspersed with incisive, wry, humorous and candid observations and commentary about the experience, his new party colleagues, rivals, and MPs, this account relates the personal story of an intensive and extraordinary four-week journey. During this time, he went from being someone with a strong knowledge of and interest in politics-but absolutely no practical experience-to becoming a Parliamentary Candidate.

With only a minimal number of days available to campaign, very little guidance, and absolutely no practical support from the under-resourced Reform UK party, this book explores the challenges and processes involved. It provides an insider's perspective on what he experienced and the varied reactions of those he encountered-be they good, bad, or ambivalent.

He was humbled and proud to play a small but important part in the party's success, winning almost 8,500 votes and an impressive 16.9% of the overall vote in his allocated constituency-behind Labour and the Conservatives. It was a result he couldn't have dreamt of just three weeks earlier, and yet he came away unjustifiably disappointed with the final outcome.

This is a serious but entertaining commentary on an intense and focused campaign, narrated in an informative yet indiscreet, engaging yet candid, and at times caustic style, which makes for easy reading. It will inform and entertain political cognoscenti and aficionados, as well as a wider audience with an interest in the machinations and personalities of a political campaign.

Thursday 6th May 2010

I was far more interested in motor racing and business and had never had any political aspirations-let alone any ambition to become an MP. However, over the course of the next few weeks, all that was to change.

I'd recently retired from a thirty-year career in the City and was ticking something off my bucket list: taking a one-week course in learning how to fly a glider. I had flown light aircraft several times before, but the prospect of not having to rely on an engine when several thousand feet in the sky was appealing. I thought it might be more reliable-not to mention safer-which, in light of what happened that bright, sunny morning, was brought into sharp focus.

Today was the day of the General Election, and if Nigel Farage's name wasn't already familiar to people from his recent performances as an MEP in the European Parliament, it certainly was after he was injured when the chartered light aircraft in which he was a passenger crash-landed at an airfield near my home in Northamptonshire. The twin-seat 'Wilga' had been towing a campaign banner reading "Vote UKIP", which got entangled in its tail fin, causing the plane to come down.

The accident resonated with me all the more because I was floating around (still under instruction) in the sky above a nearby airfield at Bicester, which brought me down to earth a little, although not literally.

Nigel Farage didn't know me from the proverbial bar of soap, I had followed his career for some years through his campaigning for Brexit and his leadership of UKIP, the latter for whom I had voted, albeit only in local elections. As he had with so many others, he made a strong impression on me, and over the years I found myself increasingly aligned with his political views.

There's no question that he's a "Marmite type of person", and you either love him or hate him-but I happen to like Marmite, and I like him, so I was definitely in the former camp when it came to sharing his views. I recognised that he could sometimes come across as intensely irritating to some, and arrogant or boorish to others. The maverick style that I was a fan of was not to everyone's taste, but I admired how he engaged with, and appeared to connect with, people of all walks of life and all ages.

Part of the persona he cultivated and regularly used to his advantage through the media-was of a man surrounded by people in a bar or outside a pub with a pint of bitter and/or a fag in hand. But that colourful and charismatic image was also genuine, something I experienced first-hand when I attended a dinner at a London club where he was promoting UKIP[1] and he bought me a pint in the bar afterwards..!

---

[1] *UKIP United Kingdom Independence Party was the Eurosceptic, populist political party in the UK, ideologically positioned on the right-wing of British*

I'm not that fickle, and this didn't influence me in any way (that would be akin to a US president being more benign about the issue of raising tariffs for UK imports as a result of being offered an unprecedented second state visit by the King!)[2] But it proved to me that he was genuine. I truly felt he would make good prime ministerial material in the future.

As I was to discover in the coming weeks, whether they liked him or not, many people viewed him as the male equivalent of the modern-day Margaret Thatcher-not just from a no-nonsense political standpoint, but also in personality. Likc her, he was forthright in his views, which were well thought out and even better articulated, and was perceived by many to be the saviour the country so badly needed. Like her, he may have been intensely disliked by some, but he was eminently electable all the same.

If nothing else, Farage was a disruptor, and that was partly what appealed to me. One of his aims was to destroy the existing political order and the two-party system. I wanted to be part of and promote the 'conversation', to unite the right and to create debate about issues that neither of

---

politics. Its emphasis was on hard Euroscepticism and was instrumental in calling for the country's exit from the EU.

[2] *In February 2025 during a televised meeting with newly inaugurated President Donald Trump, Keir Starmer handed over a personal invitation from King Charles has to make an unprecedented second state visit to the UK. He had already been hosted by Queen Elizabeth II hosted Trump on a state visit in 2019. The precedent for second-term US presidents who have already made a state visit is usually tea or lunch with the monarch as was the case for George W Bush and Barack Obama.*

the two major parties were prepared to address-yet which much of the electorate deeply cared about.

I felt that UK politicians had retreated from their values and ignored voter concerns on migration and free speech. In an era where many are frightened to speak out, he was prepared to do so-and consistently spoke more common sense than most of them put together. I felt that his philosophical courage was exciting and that he had been the single most influential and significant politician of the last ten years (including assorted Prime Ministers), and probably of our time. That was no mean achievement for someone who had never yet been an MP, despite trying to secure a seat in the House of Commons on seven previous occasions.

However, he is adept at exploiting weakness and vulnerability and is a formidable politician who had been a prominent Eurosceptic since the early 1990s. He served as an MEP from his first election in 1999 and held a very clear view of the undemocratic nature of the European Union, which he robustly challenged. He used that platform to champion Britain's exit from the EU. Without him, as the architect of Brexit, it is unlikely that the UK would ever have had a say in its membership of the European Union.

Sunday 5th May 2024

Front pages:

Sunday Times: Defeat for Street boosts Starmer's hopes of No 10

The Observer: Starmer: beaten Sunak should end purgatory of Zombie rule

Sunday Express: LAME DUCK PM LOSES TORY STRONGHOLD

Sunday Telegraph: Labour wins in West Midlands and London

A bank holiday weekend meant that drinks with friends on a Sunday evening was not quite as indulgent as it might otherwise have been. In convivial company the wine flowed and conversation naturally turned to politics, driven by the headlines dominating most of the newspapers. Talk quickly moved to who we would each vote for in the next General Election, which the media widely predicted would be held in the autumn-possibly as late as November-so still six months away.

It would be safe to say that the demographic gathered that evening consisted entirely of traditional Tory voters, all of whom had been brought up in families where successive generations had voted Conservative without question.

However, the central issue of our debate was: if not Conservative, then who?

My view was that the Tories, led by Rishi Sunak-the second unelected Prime Minister in succession-no longer resembled the party or government that we and our families had supported. After 14 years, they had broken Britain. But Labour wasn't a viable option either, for a million reasons-not least the belief that, if elected, they would bankrupt the country.

Everyone present recognised that change was needed, and that was what the electorate would ultimately be voting for. When I, somewhat warily, mooted the idea of Nigel Farage's party, Reform UK-which had evolved from his earlier platform, UKIP-I was met with what I thought was a surprisingly favourable response.

I suggested to one of my like-minded friends that I shared many of Reform's values and opinions to such an extent that I might even consider standing for them at some stage in the future. That friend, Stuart Beaty-a local farmer and landowner, like many in the farming industry soon to be massively compromised by the forthcoming Labour government-was born and bred in Northamptonshire. He had grown up with Richard Tice, whom I had met before, though he knew him far better than I did and he kindly offered to reconnect us.

At that time, no one had any idea just how soon the election would be upon us-or that the media would soon be bombarding the country with politics and election forecasts for weeks on end.

Monday 6th May

Front pages:

The Daily Telegraph: Sunak shelves summer election

The Guardian: Labour sets sights on "blue wall" seats at next election

Daily Express: ONLY BIG TAX CUTS AND GROWTH CAN SAVE TORIES NOW

The Times: UK heading for hung parliament says Sunak

Financial Times: Tories warn Sunak he needs 'vision' to repair party after poll drubbing

True to his word, and having not dismissed my comment of the previous evening as a throwaway remark, Stuart had taken the trouble to speak to Richard on my behalf and sent each of us the other's contact details.

I had always been interested in and, as a tax-paying stakeholder, engaged with domestic politics throughout my adult life. Now, like so many others, after 14 years of disastrous Tory rule that had left Britain financially and economically broken, the looming prospect of a Labour government seemed even worse. The Conservative Party-with its traditional values of lower taxation, strong borders and robust military protection, which generations of my family and I once identified with and voted for, no longer existed. The party of Churchill and Thatcher had evolved into something which was unrecognisable to me.

To say I was among a huge number of disaffected voters would be an understatement. And of course, it's in the British nature to moan about our government, especially in the run-up to an election. I felt strongly that the state of the country was such that my generation would be leaving behind an awful legacy for future generations. Like so many of my friends, I was deeply concerned-but rather than continuing to complain about politicians and the parlous state of the nation to anyone who would listen, I decided that I should either "shut up and put up", or do what most others understandably cannot or will not: get off my backside and actually try to do something about it.

I did so for the younger generations, especially on behalf of my two sons. Both in their twenties, they had already been (not only emotionally but also) financially compromised in life by the avarice of their mother from whom I was now happily divorced and, like the rest of their age group, had been completely disenfranchised by the fallout of the COVID pandemic, which severely disrupted their education, career prospects and social development. Their cohort faced the likelihood of achieving less than their parents-a trend not seen for decades-and were on course to be the first in living memory to earn less than those who came before them.

Richard Tice, who co-founded Reform UK and had personally funded much of it's operations, is passionate about the party. While less controversial and perhaps less overtly statesmanlike than Nigel Farage, he is charming, likeable, and very good company. We shared several mutual friends and had met socially on a number of occasions over the years. We are also both members of the SMTC, of which his first cousin James is president, and we had competed on the Cresta Run[3] in St. Moritz. While I knew a good deal more about him than he did about me, we were acquaintances rather than close friends.

From my perspective, he had once been more memorable for his delightful and extremely attractive ex-wife, whom he had divorced and set up home with the punchy political journalist, author and commentator Isabel Oakeshott.

Over the course of the next ten days, I had time to reflect and repeatedly asked myself if I really wanted to do this-especially in the midst of other pressing and time-consuming responsibilities, such as trying to sell my family home and other possessions in order to settle the seemingly endless financial demands from my adulterous former wife. But I felt

---

[3] *The Cresta Run is an ice track built every winter in St Moritz, Switzerland, used for "skeleton" toboggan racing. It is operated by the St. Moritz Tobogganing Club (SMTC)*

extremely strongly about the state of the country and the need to restore our national identity. I resolutely decided: yes, I did want to do this.

Having long since retired from my professional career in banking, and with both sons grown up and working in London, it was an easier decision than it might have been under different circumstances. I also resolved that, in the admittedly unlikely event of winning my seat, I was prepared to commit up to five years of my life to serve in the House of Commons, represent my constituents, and champion the policies of Reform UK. To do otherwise would have felt dishonest. That said, I had to be pragmatic and manage expectations-Reform UK was never going to win this election. It was about preparing for 2029.

Everyone who takes more than a passing interest in the politics and governance of our country has gripes and issues they're unhappy and moan about with. But now, it seemed, there were an extraordinary number of people from every demographic, young, middle-aged and older, whose lists of concerns were longer than ever, and who believed strongly that these issues needed to be addressed or reformed-with a capital R.

***

At this stage, the Prime Minister was still holding out hope for a second term in office, based on the strength of the economy and the "Rwanda plan."[4][5] But after a string of local election defeats, it was universally believed that Downing Street had shelved plans for a summer General Election, with an autumn vote now widely expected.

Thursday 16th May

Front pages:

The Times: Starmer sets out to woo voters with six pledges

Daily Mirror: KIER, MY 6 PLEDGES FOR BRITAIN

After failing to reach him on the phone, I texted Richard Tice and reminded him that we'd met before and had several mutual friends in common. I explained that it was Stuart Beaty who had given me his number with a view to

---

[4] *Isabel Oakeshott is the former Sunday Times political editor who released Matt Hancock's confidential WhatsApp messages from lockdown to The Daily Telegraph after collaborating with the former health secretary to write a book, which he described as a "massive betrayal and breach of trust"*

[5] *The Rwanda plan was a Conservative government initiative devised in 2022 to send asylum seekers to Rwanda. The plan, aimed to deter irregular migration by processing asylum claims in Rwanda instead of the UK and to relocate asylum seekers who arrived here illegally after January 2022. Under the scheme, asylum seekers would have their claims processed in Rwanda, and if successful, they'd be granted asylum and allowed to stay in the country however, the plan faced widespread criticism, especially by human rights groups and charities and was declared unlawful by the Supreme Court in November 2023, citing concerns that Rwanda was not a safe country and that asylum seekers could be at risk of ill-treatment. Legislation led to the government publishing a new treaty and introducing the Safety of Rwanda Act 2024, which declared it a safe country. The scheme was reported to have cost £700 million but only 4 people were removed under the scheme, and they did so voluntarily and was scrapped by the Labour government after the 2024 general election.*

discussing whether I could help in representing the Reform Party - which I made clear I would definitely be giving my vote to, and that I believed I could add value and credibility to.

After some 'telephone tennis', with both of us missing each other's calls, I received a message in reply in which he said that he was hugely grateful and appreciative of my offer of help and support.

Showing that he is a man after my own heart, and of great taste, he also complimented me on the "nice cars - petrol, of course" shown in my WhatsApp profile photo.

Friday 17th May

Front pages:

Daily Express: BE WARNED! TAXES WILL GO UP UNDER LABOUR, WARNS HUNT

The Daily Telegraph: LABOUR TAX RISES AS SURE AS NIGHT FOLLOWS DAY, SAYS HUNT

The Independent: Starmer dons his boots in election battleground

Financial Times: Starmer lays cards on table

Despite repeated and failed attempts throughout the day to speak to Richard, we agreed to try and reconnect next week. I then left home for the long drive up to the Lincolnshire Wolds, where I was due to compete in a pair of motor races at the Cadwell Park circuit over the course of the weekend.

Sunday 19th May

After an enjoyable and relatively successful weekend's racing, the drive back home to Northamptonshire was even longer and more arduous due to interminable traffic jams caused by contraflows and needless diversions for road works - which could only have existed in the imagination of the local councils, as there was no evidence of any repairs or related activity.

However, it did give me a few hours to ruminate and seriously consider where I stood and whether I really wanted to do this.

Up until now, I'd not had any direct involvement in politics, even at a local level, but I had met several politicians over the years. One of my early memories was of my parents going to see the wartime Prime Minister Winston Churchill lying in state at Westminster - but only because they left me behind at home, thinking I was too young to go with them.

My first contact with a politician was limited to shaking hands with the former PM Edward Heath as a thirteen-year-old when he visited my school to deliver some sort of lecture. However, apart from being aware that he had recently been Prime Minister, he made no more of an impression on me than would the secretary of the local golf club - and in fact, that was exactly the sort of person he reminded me of.

Sadly, the closest I ever got to my political hero, Margaret Thatcher, was appearing on a Capital Radio phone-in programme with her wayward son, Mark[6] at a time when we were both competing for sponsorship to fund our respective careers as racing drivers.

Over the years, I had made small donations to the Conservative Party, as a result of which I was due to be placed next to Tory party leader William Hague[7] at a fundraising dinner. I was, however, grateful that he had to cancel his appearance at the last minute and his wife, Ffion, took his place, which pleased me, as she was extremely good company and considerably better looking than him!

When he was a relatively new MP, I had also met the then-future PM David (by now the strategically ennobled Lord) Cameron[8] at dinner parties and although he was

---

[6] *Mark Thatcher is son of the former PM who achieved notoriety in 1982 when he, his co-driver and mechanic went missing for several days when competing on the Paris-Dakar rally.*

[7] *Lord William Hague was Leader of the Conservative Party from 1997 - 2001*

[8] *Sir Edward Heath won the 1970 election for the Conservative Party, and served his only term as Prime Minister during a time of strong industrial*

amiable company, I later marvelled at the wisdom of having no business or work experience outside of Westminster.

However, one of the most likeable and charismatic politicians I had contact with was the MP Sir David Davis, who'd lost the Conservative Party leadership contest to Cameron in 2005. I spent a great day with him in the summer of 2009 when we travelled down to watch the recording of the BBC's *Top Gear* TV show at Dunsfold Aerodrome, together with a mutual friend - who, like David, knew racing driver Ben Collins (aka 'The Stig'), as they'd all previously served as SAS reservists.

Thanks to Ben's kind invitation, we were lucky enough to see World Champion racing driver Michael Schumacher performing as the 'Star in the Reasonably Priced Car', although the highlight for me was David insisting on asking for Jeremy Clarkson's autograph on behalf of my sons - as Jeremy and I had previously exchanged sharp words at a prior event at Goodwood.

David later bought drinks for the three of us on the way home but, mindful of the furore created by the parliamentary

---

upheaval and economic decline during which he led Britain into the European Community. He pursued a number of policies that would later become identified with 'Thatcherism' although he was an outspoken critic of Margaret Thatcher.

expenses scandal that had emerged earlier that year[9] he was at great pains to stress that he'd paid for this out of his own pocket!

The nearest I'd got to front-line politics was meeting the former Conservative leader John Major[10], who in my view is one of the most maligned and underrated PMs of all time.[11] I first met him in the late 1980s when, still in office, he opened our company's new HQ in the city. We met again in the 2000s when he was a consultant to Credit Suisse and we hosted a reception for investors and clients in Hong Kong.

---

[9] *The Parliamentary expenses scandal that emerged in 2009, concerned expense claims made by politicians over previous years. It uncovered serial misuse of expenses and allowances by MPs and led to widespread anger among the public which resulted in a large number of sackings, resignations, and de-selections together with the repayment of expenses totaling £1.3million. These ranged from a tin of dog food, to a light bulb, to £90,000 spent on the upkeep of an MP's country estate but was symbolized by an ornamental duck house by Tory MP Sir Peter Viggers. It also led to the creation of the Independent Parliamentary Standards Authority (IPSA) which ended the self-regulation of MPs' pay and expenses.*

[10] *John Major served in Margaret Thatcher's government and after a cabinet reshuffle became Chancellor of the Exchequer in 1989. When Thatcher unexpectedly resigned in November 1990, he found himself in pole position to contend for the leadership of the Conservative Party and also the position of prime minister. With Thatcher's unofficial support, Major won a three-way contest for the leadership and so became prime minister in November, 1990.In April 1992, in the first general elections after his ascendancy, the Conservatives won, which confirmed his leadership.*

[11] *Lord David Cameron became the youngest Prime Minister in 198 years in 2010 when the Conservatives and Liberal Democrats formed a coalition government. He continued as Prime Minister from May 2015 until July 2016 leading a Conservative government. He was elevated to the House of Lords in 2023*

He had struck a chord with me when he once said, “Only in Britain could it be thought a defect to be ‘too clever by half’. The probability is that too many people are too stupid by three quarters.”

To my surprise, one of the best public speakers I’d ever come across at a dinner hosted by my bank was actually Ken Livingstone, the ultra-left-wing leader of the GLC and later Mayor of London, who delivered a remarkably apolitical and inspiring speech but it is Nigel Farage who’d made the most significant impression on me, in the way he was prepared to challenge conventional wisdom and his dislike of received opinion and spoke passionately of the need to win back the disillusioned right wing voters.

Tuesday 21st May

At Stuart’s suggestion, I decided to trek up to the Rutland County Museum in Oakham, where Tice was speaking and introducing Chris Clowes as Reform’s local PPC for the constituency.

Whenever I see a collection of white vans (they are always white and never operate in isolation) with the words *‘Highways Maintenance’* emblazoned on their flanks, I always think it a contradiction in terms. They are usually encircled and protected by a fortress of temporary plastic street furniture, and ‘washroom facilities’ for non-existent operatives littering some of our most important and busy roads and routes. Yet they are invariably unattended, with no sign of activity, plant, or workmen- and least of all, any sign of *maintenance*. With their strategically positioned cones and uncoordinated and illogically positioned traffic lights directing the seemingly endless queues of vehicles that they have caused, they appear to exist solely to create myriad and completely unnecessary diversions, adding misery and mayhem for disgruntled motorists.

Having battled my way through the resultant traffic jams to get there, I arrived too late to hear Chris speak - but just in time for Richard. I was keen to see how well he came across in front of a live audience, and to get a sense of the demographic and gauge their reaction.

I had no concern on the former, as I already knew that Richard is debonair, extremely plausible, and a well-practised, slick performer. In line with my expectations - and predictably - there didn't seem to be anyone present under the age of fifty. But there were several women, and somewhat to my surprise, the attendance definitely wasn't just pale, male, and stale.

The reaction of the sixty or so people there was very friendly and largely supportive. There were a lot of questions, all of which he answered with great aplomb and genuine conviction.

I was surprised to have to pay for the privilege of attending and, as I was yet to learn how underfunded the party was, I rather innocently hoped that the entry fee was a donation to the excellent museum. But, as entry to that was free, I assumed that was not the case.

I spoke briefly to Richard before I left, and we agreed to talk the following morning - but neither of us anticipated what was to happen the next day.

Wednesday 22nd May

I had to make another unnecessary online court appearance with my ex-wife, which was rightly dismissed by the long-suffering judge as a needless waste of everyone's money as well as precious court time. It represented a pyrrhic victory for me but once again raised my stress levels and consumed yet more of my energy-at a point when I could least afford it.

However, the day suddenly became even more memorable when Rishi Sunak, our Prime Minister, called a snap election. My quest to become a PPC suddenly took on a different complexion and far greater urgency.

I messaged Richard to confirm my interest in going through the screening or vetting process, whatever that might entail. I had visions of some sort of Masonic ceremony taking place in a darkened lodge where I'd be interviewed under caution and have to swear a lifetime allegiance to the party and its leader, on pain of death, before qualifying to become a PPC.

However, I was concerned that today's surprise announcement may have thwarted all that and would leave us all, especially me, with such a small window and too little time to make a meaningful impression. Due to the numerous bureaucratic hurdles that I was to encounter, I would actually be left with far less time than even the six weeks' notice that Rishi's announcement had given the other candidates to prepare.

To the contrary, however, Richard's immediate and encouraging response was that it wasn't too late, and that I should apply online *ASAP*, as the party needed "good people"... It all seemed a bit too easy.

My naïve and uneducated assumption was that it would be logical for me to be allocated the constituency of South Northamptonshire, where I lived. A subsequent conversation with Richard suggested that it could be available. It was a Conservative seat, and the high-profile, well-respected and personable Tory MP Andrea Leadsom, whom I not only knew socially but also respected and liked very much indeed, was the incumbent.

She was an excellent MP who had been a contender for party leadership in 2016 and would be unbeatable opposition, although it would have been a great honour to be on the same ballot paper as someone I had willingly voted for in the past. Of course, I also had a lot of connections and points of contact in the local community. Unfortunately, that was to be a short-lived dream.

***

With Labour currently 21 points ahead in the opinion polls, it had been a widely held belief that the election would be called for either late October or early November. But Rishi Sunak, had announced a snap election to take place on 4th July, thus ending months of speculation on when he would do so.

Already isolated within his own party, the beleaguered and bedraggled Prime Minister looked a forlorn and very sorry figure as he stood in front of the steps of Number 10 Downing Street in the pouring rain. Despite the weather forecast predicting very heavy rain, Rishi completely ignored the warning and elected (possibly not the best choice of word) not to use the sanctuary of an umbrella-getting thoroughly drenched as a result.

More importantly, he also completely ignored the advice of his election campaign director, Isaac Levido, who had told him to delay the General Election until the autumn.

The portrayal he unwittingly gave seemed to sum up the mood of both the country and the Conservative Party, who were widely expected to lose after 14 years in power.

"Now is the moment for Britain to choose its future," he proclaimed to the baying and sodden journalists and TV crews, as he listed the very few highlights and even shorter list of his achievements during his tenure in government, which began and ended with his furlough scheme during the Covid lockdown. He returned to the front door looking as though he'd been standing in a shower cubicle fully clothed for at least ten minutes. It was a sad image and marked the beginning of the end of his tenure as (unelected) PM, but proved a delight to headline writers whose quips included: *"It never rains but it pours," "Things will only get wetter,"* and more inevitably, *"Wally without a Brolly."*

It was the first of several more gaffes yet to come, but the image was a portent of bad omens ahead of the party suffering the worst defeat in its history.

He was taking a huge risk, which was hard to fathom but part of the logic behind his premature timing appeared to be some good news in the form of GDP figures, which indicated a return to economic growth, together with a dramatic drop in inflation data, which had fallen to 2.3% in the previous month. In doing so, he was gambling that these were as good as they were going to get-although it seemed an ill-advised and uneducated stab in the dark for someone who had previously been Chancellor. Not only was the economic data expected to improve still further over the course of the year-but it did.

Rishi was also taking an over-optimistic view that the previously mentioned Rwanda deportation scheme was just about to become law and finally take off together with the aeroplanes which he hoped would contain hordes of immigrants. He believed that together, these would provide a sufficient boost to his popularity and give him the best chance of re-election and a return to Number 10.

However, a significant incentive for Sunak's timing was the threat posed by the 'Farage Factor' which he was very much alive to. Nigel had previously made it clear that he was going to help his friend and ally, the unpredictable former US President Donald Trump (poetically described by Labour as a "Tyrant in a Toupee") in the forthcoming presidential elections, which were scheduled for November. This would therefore preclude Nigel from standing for the Reform Party that he had founded.

The prospect of the Reform Party taking a significant number of votes away from the Tories was a real threat, which the PM felt needed to be removed from the equation. The recognition of this was a backhanded compliment to the party.

It appeared that Sunak's gamble might have paid off in that respect, as Farage initially made it clear that he would not be standing as a candidate, although he did stress that he would actively help and support the efforts of his candidates. While this promise of assistance was welcomed, it represented a hammer blow of disappointment to the young party and its growing pool of candidates-but would have come as a great relief to the PM, as it appeared that at least that part of his questionable strategy had come good.

Thursday 23rd May

Front pages:

Daily Express: PM: I am fighting for our nation's future

i: Judgement day: 4th July: Snap election for UK

The Times: Sunak bets the house

The Daily Telegraph: Sunak gambles on snap poll

Daily Mirror: Drown and out

Daily Mail: Now is the moment for Britain to choose its future

The Guardian: Sunak's big gamble

Financial Times: Sunak bets on July 4th election

Metro: Rishi finally sets date for poll. ELECTION: July4th

I took Richard up on his strict instruction to complete the application to be a PPC (Prospective Parliamentary

Candidate), but first, I obviously had to sign up and become a member of the party. Despite my strong convictions, I had never previously been a member of any political party before, but shelled out the requisite £25 to become one for the first time in my life.

I next turned my attention to filling in the candidacy form which, although quite lengthy, seemed straightforward enough. Little did I know that this would not be my first attempt at completing it.

Separately, I was then asked to attach a further £25 to my application, which I assumed was some sort of 'processing' fee - for which, in retrospect, I should have asked to be refunded, such was the organisation's inability to process it in an efficient or timely fashion.

Whilst I assumed that my credentials would be rigorously checked as part of the vetting process, I was comfortable in the knowledge that I had no hidden skeletons in the cupboard. However, I was still amazed at the ease with which anyone could apparently apply to represent what, even though it had metamorphosed and grown out of Nigel Farage's previous entity, UKIP, was essentially a start-up. It was not a surprise when it later became clear that some less than suitable applicants had slipped through the net.

Indeed, when I attended a "rally" nine months later, I went through a far more rigorous process before, even as a paid-up member of the party, I was screened for my suitability to attend and allowed to be relieved of £3 to buy an entry ticket..!

My smug satisfaction at having completed the requisite online paperwork was immediately dampened when, in the case of "The computer says no," the clunky system steadfastly refused to register my application. It took several more attempts before it finally even acknowledged receipt. Having now done this three times, I tried to comfort myself with the ridiculous notion that, if all three of the individual applications had been registered separately, then it might give me a greater chance of being selected!

Despite the urgency of the situation, it would take even longer before my application was screened - if indeed it ever was - and finally confirmed. In the meantime, having completed it several times, it brought to mind what appears to have become accepted standard practice, which I've never understood: so many forms that one has to fill in these days require us to declare, without question, whether we are gay, straight, or identify ourselves as, or are assigned with, anything other than the gender into which we have been born.

I may be old-fashioned in that respect, but I'm a firm believer that there are only two biological sexes, and that if you castrate your dog, it doesn't mean that he suddenly becomes a bitch, in the same way that if a man has a sex change, he is still going to have to undergo an all-important prostate examination at some point in his/her life. Adam and Eve would have been so bewildered that they'd probably never have "got together" had they been instructed to create and accommodate as many as the 72 sexes that society is being brainwashed into believing now exist in order to appease the minorities.

Hence, I'm in complete agreement with the view that former MEP and subsequent Reform MP, Rupert Lowe,[12] would subsequently express: "There are two sexes: female and male. People shouldn't be afraid to say so. It is confusing and potentially dangerous to cloud that. We must respect everyone's individual choices, and everyone is free to live as they choose, but that does not change scientific reality."

In any case, I felt that my sexual proclivities should be no business of anyone other than myself and my partner (in itself a ghastly and ambiguous term), and nor should my religion, race, or the shade or colour of my skin be of the slightest relevance in any context whatsoever.

---

[12] *Rupert Lowe: At the 2019 European Parliament election, he was elected as MEP for the West Midlands, representing the Brexit Party, which later became Reform UK. He entered Parliament at the 2024 general election for Reform MP for Great Yarmouth but the whip was suspended in March 2025 due to legal accusations.*

I find it curious that, in the Orwellian world of “Big Brother” in which we exist, we have become increasingly accustomed to operating like this and blindly accepting of answering fatuous questions which demand us to impart ever more personal details, including religious belief, ethnicity, and date of birth.

I'm one of those who already dislike the ridiculous practice, imported from our friends in America, of having to spell out my rather cumbersome name for the barista in the local ‘Fuckoffee’ (yes, it really does exist...) shop, only to have it misheard, incorrectly transcribed onto the side of the polystyrene cup, and mispronounced as it's shouted out at the top of their voice across the floor. I've lost count of the number of times that I've had to resist the temptation of providing them with a cartoon character name like "Mickey Mouse" or the even easier to pronounce “Mike Hunt”, which might deter them from this ridiculous practice.

I wonder how long it will be before we are all obliged to provide some of this intrusive personal data before our orders for a ‘flat white’ or one of its many variants is accepted?

***

On his first day of campaigning, the PM visited a brewery in Wales where he met with an awkward silence and was subsequently mocked when he tactlessly asked if people were looking forward to the upcoming Euro 2024 football tournament, oblivious to the fact that Wales hadn't actually qualified for it.

Of more importance, it became clear that there were a handful of 'insiders' who were privy to Sunak's decision to go to the country as early as he did and, using this information, had already placed bets on the timing of the election ahead of the announcement, something that would later come back to bite Rishi where it hurts. However, almost everyone else was caught completely off guard, not least most of his own MPs, who, like everyone else including the raft of new PPCs across all the other parties, now had only six weeks to rally troops and organise their respective election campaigns.

Most of the exhausted and demoralised Tory MPs felt that a summer election would be suicidal and, unlike most things they'd had to opine on whilst in office, they were to be proved correct. Indeed, the former Tory chairman Jake Berry was outspoken and blunt in making his views crystal clear when he said that these figures showed the decision to call an early election was "one of the most stupid political misjudgements in the history of politics".

With decades of healthy funding from the trade unions, Labour were of course by far and away the best funded, with a well-organised infrastructure that was ready and poised to swing into action at a moment's notice. The Conservatives had far fewer paid-up members, but they too had a well-practised campaign machine and a very well-established network with huge resources on which to rely.

Conversely, Reform had fewer than 30,000 paid-up members before the campaign, although this would double to more than 60,000 by the time of the election. However, they were still a very young party and, whilst benefactors such as Richard Tice himself and later Zia Yusuf and Nick Candy[13] had invested some of their own wealth, the fledgling party lacked the financial wherewithal and organisation of both the main protagonists, as well as those of the Lib Dems and even the Greens who could no longer be dismissed as the party of 'sprout lovers' from Islington.

It would become increasingly evident that we were all completely unprepared for the campaign ahead.

---

[13] *Zia Yusuf is a former investment banker and millionaire entrepreneur who founded a luxury concierge company which was sold to private equity in 2023 after which he turned to politics. Having made a significant financial donation to the party in June 2024, he spoke at a Reform UK rally, in Birmingham and the following month, he succeeded Richard Tice as Chairman of Reform UK. He is in charge of day-to-day operations and has overseen a drive to professionalise the party. He dispensed with "old hands" such as communications chief Gawain Towler and also moved the party's HQ from a sleepy town in Leicestershire to Millbank Tower in London.*
Nick Candy is a billionaire property developer and former donor to the Conservatives but is now Reform's treasurer. He has personally pledged a seven-figure sum to the party and although he has no operational involvement in it has spearheaded a fundraising drive among wealthy donors.

Friday 24th May

Front pages:

The Times: Energy bills tumble in first big election battle

The Daily Telegraph: Starmer lacks the courage to debate me, says Sunak

Daily Mail: Tories to cut green levies on fuel bills

Daily Mirror: ELECTION: BAD START FOR SUNAK

i: Smoking ban dropped as snap election also stops help to renters

Guardian: Sunak begins election campaign by dropping flagship policies

Daily Express: PM's plan to 'take down' Starmer in TV debates

Daily Star: The GENERAL EJECTION

The Independent: It never rains but it pours, Rishi, so you'll need one of these

Financial Times: Sunak makes faltering election start after Rwanda and smoking setbacks

Metro: RISHI'S BUMPY TAKE-OFF

I had received an immediate automated confirmation email that I had become a member of the party from HQ, and another one welcoming me to the party from Paul

Hogan, the PPC for the constituency that I lived in, which was very efficient. I took up his invitation to call him and introduce myself.

Paul, I would later find out, was a genuinely nice fellow who did a great job for the party in what historically was a very strongly held Conservative constituency, but he was rather defensive when I somewhat tactlessly mentioned that I was also intending to stand. Although I stressed that I had not been allocated South Northants, his mood changed, and I felt that he was, quite understandably, somewhat guarded in his enthusiasm for me. It was probably not the best start to have made with someone who was destined to become an ally and one of my valued colleagues over the course of the next few weeks.

I told Richard that I'd spoken to Paul earlier and that he'd confirmed he would continue to stand for the constituency which, although disappointing from my perspective, I said would probably rule me out of contention. As ever the optimist, however, Richard was encouraging and insisted that it would not.

***

Once again, Sunak showed his affinity to water and followed up his soaking outside Number 10 by scoring another own goal - this time by visiting the site where the Titanic was built before it sank in 1912. There he faced the obvious question from a journalist, which was on everyone's mind given that his party was 28 points behind in the polls: *"We are just yards from where the Titanic was built. Are you captaining a sinking ship going into this election?"*

It also led to captions citing his problems as being "Titanic", references to his "Titanic errors in judgment", and memes that cheekily lifted the letter 'A' away from his name so that it simply read "SUNK"

Commenting on his decision to call the election when he did, Sunak had reportedly told his cabinet - in the cringing and unconvincing style of Del Boy Trotter from the TV series *Only Fools and Horses* - "he who dares wins". However, an unprecedented number of his own MPs were voting with their feet and didn't dare to stay on that particular, and now rapidly sinking, ship when it went down.

Putting loyalties (if indeed there were any) to one side, if a ship is sinking it doesn't much matter who is the captain.

To date, 120 MPs had declared that they wouldn't be standing again, of which an unprecedented 78 were Conservatives, thus beating the unwanted record of the 75 who stood down ahead of the 1997 election. It wasn't just a protest against Sunak's leadership but simply recognition that the party was facing a bloodbath.

A number of those who might not have been ready to move away from politics were jumping before they were pushed out by the electorate in an act of reputational damage limitation. Another deciding factor was Labour's proposed ban on second jobs for MPs, which was likely to cost the Conservatives rather more than Labour.

The exodus was led by Michael Gove, former PM Theresa May and Dame Andrea Leadsom, who were joined by several other former cabinet ministers. The opportunities are fewer in opposition, and the pay outside Westminster is more lucrative after all.

Saturday 25th May

Front pages

Daily Telegraph: Inheritance tax against Tory values, says Hunt

The Times: Gove quits politics as more Tories stand down

i Weekend: Gove quits as Sunak hit by record exodus of Tory MPs

Daily Express: NOW GOVERNMENT QUITS! MINISTER'S SHOCK EXIT ROCKS TORIES

Daily Mirror: NOW GOVE QUITS SUNAK'S SINKING SHIP

Daily Mail: BORIS: Starmer would be the most dangerous and Left-wing Labour PM since the 1970s

Reeves: I'LL NEVER PLAY FAST AND LOOSE WITH YOUR MONEY

FT Weekend: Gove quits as Tory pre-election exodus pushes past 1997 flight

The news that the Conservative candidate for my home constituency of South Northamptonshire, Andrea Leadsom, was one of those standing down convinced me that, despite it being a traditional Tory stronghold, this would be where I might stand the greatest chance of success. I had lived there for thirty years and was confident that I'd have a lot of resonance and traction with the electorate, both socially through my network of friends and with the myriad of local businesses that I had exposure to thanks to my involvement in the world of motorsport.

Whilst this was being considered, the selection committee, if indeed it ever got that far, had confirmed that they had quite rightly decided to leave Paul in place. So, as that potential option was definitely closed down, Richard suggested that I speak to Sean Lever, who was the Northamptonshire area coordinator, about the possibility of taking on the Daventry constituency instead.

This idea didn't fill me with joy and was one which I initially rejected as, apart from anything else, it was a much less appealing prospect from a logistical point of view. However, over the course of the next week, I reasoned with and ultimately convinced myself that, although the town itself wasn't exactly on my doorstep, I did actually have quite a few friends in the constituency who I could rely on for support and help, as well as exposure to racing teams, suppliers and engineering companies. So, whilst it was not my first choice, it wasn't as impractical and unrealistic as it might have first seemed.

***

From a personal view, I was disappointed not to have had the opportunity to challenge Andrea but was also sad that she was standing down, as she had been an excellent MP for our constituency. She had, amongst other things, campaigned tirelessly and railed against (another very bad pun?!) the over-budget, behind-schedule and increasingly unnecessary and extremely costly white elephant that is HS2.[14] Like many others, I felt she still had so much more to offer in Parliament.

The benefit of the democratic system in our country is that it allows anyone with a few exceptions such as

---

[14] HS2 is a project to build a high-speed rail line in England. Originally planned to connect London to Birmingham, Manchester, Leeds and York but in October 2023, PM Rishi Sunak cancelled the line north of the West Midlands due to spiraling cost overruns, delays and changes to post-covid travel.

bankrupts and overpaid, all too powerful, civil servants (many of whom could be described as morally bankrupt) to put their heads above the parapet, as I had done, and choose to become an elected representative for people in a given constituency.

There are downsides of course: in the US, the minimum age for a senator is 30 years old, whereas in the UK, one only needs to be 18 to be an MP, which is far too young. You don't even need to be on the electoral roll and, other than being a British citizen, there are very few qualifications. It seems ludicrous that potentially someone who has never been a taxpayer (preferably for several years) can properly represent those who have.

Apart from the fact that there are far too many MPs in this country, an additional problem is that we do not pay them enough and, as a result, don't attract the brightest and finest brains. This means that the people most capable of running the country are disincentivised and, anyway, far too smart to get into politics in the first place. You will always get what you pay for and, as the saying goes, "if you pay peanuts, you'll get monkeys." And yet, being in government includes some of the most important and crucial jobs in the country although, perversely, it is one of the very few roles for which you don't need any training or qualifications, as the impending Labour government was to prove so comprehensively.

Unlike many of her Westminster contemporaries, and all those in the forthcoming Labour cabinet, Andrea Leadsom had already had a long and distinguished business career before she became an MP. However, an example of the paucity of talent in Parliament was future Deputy PM Angela Rayner who, like the majority of the incoming Labour cabinet, had little or no experience of working in the private sector, running a business, or creating any economic value.

Rayner had left school early and without any academic qualifications, becoming a single mother at the age of 16 before training to work in social care - which is laudable - during which time she became a trade union representative. But it's stretching the imagination to comprehend just what she brings to the table of high office.

Judging by her questionable taste in often ill-fitting clothes, topped off with a fringe that looked as though it had been trimmed by her own grandmother, she at least appeared to have a self-deprecating sense of humour - but so do many comedians, and that doesn't necessarily make them suitably qualified to be politicians.

The larger-than-life Rayner, or "Grangela" as she nicknamed herself when she became the youngest grandmother in the House of Commons at the age of 37, told stories against herself of how she'd attempted to distract Boris Johnson's notoriously wandering eyes at PMQs in the style of the film *Fatal Attraction*, when she emulated the actress Sharon Stone by crossing and uncrossing her legs and flashing what the flame-haired Deputy Party Leader crudely described to other MPs as her "ginger growler".

One of my constituents rather cruelly likened a televised interview with her discussing the economy to watching a hamster trying to respond to questions about quantum physics. I didn't see it myself but certainly saw a similarity to some of the caricatures portrayed in the *Little Britain* TV series.

It was her eclectic dress sense and garishly coloured wardrobe - some of which it emerged she didn't pay for - that made her stand out from the crowd. However, as with the hapless. Often tongue-tied and mathematically innumerate former Shadow Home Secretary Diane[15] ("Abacus") Abbott it is difficult to take "No-brainer Rayner" seriously. The prospect of her becoming any part of our government, let alone the Deputy PM as she was destined, was both as

---

[15] *Diane Abbott (MP for Hackney North and Stoke Newington since 1987. She served in the Shadow Cabinet of Jeremy Corbyn as Shadow Home Secretary from 2016 to 2020 She was the first black woman elected to parliament and is the longest-serving black MP, and since 2024 the longest continually serving female MP making her the "Mother of the House"*

offensive and laughable as a sketch from the satirical TV show.

Sunday 26th May

Front pages

Sunday Express: RISHI: I'LL BRING IN NATIONAL SERVICE

Sunday Times: Tory plan for all 18-year-olds to do National Service

The Mail on Sunday: RISHI: I'LL BRING BACK NATIONAL SERVICE

The Sunday Telegraph: PM: I'll bring back National Service

The Observer: Reeves slams 'reckless' Sunak over £64bn tax cut pledges

I had checked with my credit card provider that both payments of £25 had been debited and, whilst I'd now been confirmed as a fully paid-up member of a political party for the first time in my life - although my membership card didn't actually arrive until nine months later, and whether by design or not, that was on April Fools' Day 2025 - I was concerned that I'd yet to receive any acknowledgement that my application for candidacy had actually been received.

However, I took comfort in the fact that, despite making payments totaling £50, it wasn't a sum that would break the bank, and nor would I begrudge the contribution to the party, even if nothing more was to come of it.

Settling down to watch the weekend of sport, which included the Monaco Grand Prix and the FA Cup Final, provided time to reflect on the PM's curious timing of the election, which seemed unnecessarily risky and was curious for other reasons too. Sunak would have been well aware that it not only fell at the start of the British summer holiday season, but would also clash with the Football Euros and would fall in the middle of the Wimbledon Tennis Championships, both of which might distract people and divert their attention away from the election.

If that was part of a deliberate ploy, then it was difficult to understand the logic behind it. Perhaps he thought Andy Murray and the England football team would be well en route to their respective finals (he was wrong on the former but, uncharacteristically, correct on the latter). Was he really hoping that the electorate would be so intoxicated and distracted by the country's sporting prowess that they wouldn't want to change anything - not even their government - due to a possible feel-good factor permeating the country?

With his track record, no one could be quite sure what was in his mind, but his decision suggested that he and his coterie hadn't thought it through properly. The electorate had a right to be dismayed and disgusted with the Conservatives, who had lost their trust by rewarding them with a complete breach of their election promises. The country absolutely did want change - and that's what it was going to be voting for.

***

On the subject of TV, Anita Singh in *The Daily Telegraph* was later to write that we should "forget the televised debates and party manifestos, the most revealing thing the party leaders did in the run-up to the UK election was to tell *Radio Times* what TV they'd enjoyed recently."

Rishi Sunak plumped for *Bridgerton*, "fatally unaware" that Regency England as a "multicultural wonderland" might not chime with the Tory base. Nigel Farage chose *Baby Reindeer*, the year's "most unapologetically controversial" series. Keir Starmer, ever keen to conceal his plans from voters, "dodged the question entirely".

Monday 27th May

Front pages:

Financial Times: Sunak steps up National Service push as campaign stutters stir Tory dismay

Daily Mail: RISHI FIGHTS BACK AS HIS NATIONAL SERVICE PLAN IS RIDICULED

The Times: Labour: We will act fast to win trust on security

The Guardian: Sunak's national service plan is 'bonkers', says ex-military chief

Daily Mirror: TORIES' LATEST BARMY PLAN. DESPERATE

Daily Telegraph: Young Royals face National Service in Sunak plan

i: Labour plan to rebuild Britain will rely on private finance

I received an email from Reform's Membership team thanking me for my support and attaching a certificate of membership, which concluded with an ambiguous and grammatically incorrect, strange slogan proclaiming, "Let's go do something extraordinary!" The underwhelming experience so far was proving to be something less than that.

What I really wanted, though, was a response to the multiple emails that I had now sent to the candidates team, in the absence of which I had more time for reflection on the stance I was taking. I was very clear in my mind that if anyone voted Labour, they would get Labour, but also that those who voted Conservative would also get Labour. It was not an appealing prospect, but I was not prepared to reward

Labour with my vote for the failure and incompetence of the Tories. I felt strongly that there was very little to differentiate the two. Reform UK offered a viable alternative and one that, come the next General Election in 2029-or hopefully sooner-was likely to become the opposition to the next Labour government.

With the geopolitical situation and conflict raging in both Ukraine and the Middle East, I reasoned that I would much rather have Nigel Farage running the country in the event of a war than Sunak, Starmer, and certainly, God forbid, Rayner or Reeves. Reform is what the country needed in so many respects but also what the Conservatives needed to put the right wing back into them. Our party did not want to become a graveyard for washed-up Tory MPs, but I fully expected that several of them would transfer their allegiance in the years following the forthcoming election.

***

In the meantime, whilst the country was still digesting the announcement of the snap election and bracing itself for six weeks of non-stop media coverage of manifestos, more broken promises, lip service, dirty tricks, and character assassination, people were already forming views on the two main protagonists.

The Tories had suffered the consequences of a rotating leadership. Liz Truss[16] had not been voted for by the electorate and was famous not only for the damage she did to the economy in record-breaking time but also because she had been the shortest-serving PM in history, managing to defy gravity for the embarrassingly short time of 49 days- which could hardly even be defined as 'work experience' let alone an apprenticeship. She would have been grateful that she didn't take much more than her toothbrush and overnight bag into her temporary residence of Number 10 because she wouldn't have had enough time to unpack too many suitcases. Her brief tenure of premiership was such that it was likened to the shelf life of an "iceberg lettuce" by the tabloid press.

It also prompted a series of wry but pertinent jokes, including one which suggested that she would have to fly first class for the rest of her life because no one would want her anywhere near either business or (the) economy.

Rishi Sunak was the latest unelected PM, who no one outside the Conservative Party had voted for either, and had inherited not only the legacy of the party's previous terms in

---

[16] *Liz Truss held various Cabinet positions under three Conservative Prime Ministers before taking over the role herself together with leadership of the Conservative Party from September to October 2022. On her fiftieth day in office, she stepped down from office making her the shortest-serving PM in British history.*

office but also the mess that his predecessor had left him. Small of stature and described by some of the female electorate as being quite sweet and with a certain school boyish charm, he came across as someone likeable enough, who had been a reasonable Chancellor in his previous role and would have been better placed to have remained, but was out of his depth as an ineffectual PM.

Likened in appearance by some to 'Mowgli', the fictional but sweet and endearing character in Rudyard Kipling's *Jungle Book*, it was difficult not to feel some empathy for a man who would have known that he could not win and was simply throwing in the towel early in order to get the inevitable out of the way as soon as possible.

More fluent in speech than his opposite number, he displayed some of the qualities of a crowd-pleaser but critically not the ability to actually please a crowd. He was falling on his sword to some extent but, as he was to discover to his cost, Britain tends not to forgive its politicians, and he was set to make several unforgivable mistakes over the course of the next few weeks.

However, like the leader of the opposition, he simply lacked plausibility, and the public perception of the fortune that he and his multi-millionaire heiress wife had at their disposal would always work against him. This led to people thinking that, as with Starmer, he was out of touch with reality and therefore the people he was representing. The Tories had become dysfunctional, and the party had alienated too many existing and potential voters. Voting against them was far more attractive than voting for them, and after all, if people are going to vote, then they want to feel good about it-even if it's irrational.

Keir Starmer had already shown that he was muddled about how a woman should be defined and his unconvincing approach was to try and make a virtue out of being working class, and even though King Charles is someone who works, the Labour leader was later to struggle to define what he thought 'working class' actually meant. He repeatedly referred to the fact that he was the son of a toolmaker, which led to predictable comparisons which suggested that he was the biggest and most glaringly obvious example of his father's products.

He espoused the politics of envy and appeared to take the view that anyone who was remotely successful and had made money from their own efforts was 'guilty' of not being "working class", in itself a misnomer. Unless, of course, they were footballers at his favoured club, Arsenal, who earned many hundreds of thousands of pounds each week, yet were deified as the acceptable face of capitalism for some reason. Everything about him smacked of hypocrisy, and he lived up to the sobriquet that a friend of mine had given him: "Bad Karma Starmer".

Lucy Allan became the latest of a wave of MPs to stand down from the Conservative Party, in her case to support the Reform UK candidate, Alan Adams, in the Telford seat that she was vacating, saying that he would offer an alternative to "more of the same politics and more of the same politicians". By this time, most of the beleaguered Tory MPs who hadn't yet stood down weren't thinking as far ahead as that but were simply fighting to keep their jobs in the short term.

Tuesday 28th May

Front pages:

Daily Express: I'M ON YOUR SIDE! PM PLEDGES BUMPER PENSION RISE

i: Labour mayors warn Starmer: we will fight for better deal

Daily Mail: FOUR IN TEN TO QUIT PRIVATE SCHOOL UNDER KEIR'S TAX

The Times: City figures back Labour with call for new outlook

The Independent: Now it gets personal: Voters like and trust Keir more than Rishi

Daily Mirror: STARMER TELLS VOTERS YOU CAN END TORY CHAOS

Daily Telegraph: PM: State pensions will never be taxed

Metro: SIR KEIR: MY ROCKY START IN LIFE

My day started with yet another friendly and welcoming, but inept, email from Reform (they were good with these), this time from the East Midlands Area Manager, Helen O'Hare. It was laden with platitudes about Reform and its intentions; however, it was addressed to me as a new party member, which suggested that she had no idea that, like her, I was hoping to become a PC.

Annoyingly, there was still no acknowledgement from the understaffed candidates' team as to whether my application had been received, let alone processed, screened, rejected or approved, which was unsatisfactory. I presumed that they were inundated with requests from hopefuls like me, but the lack of communication was really frustrating as it was out of my control and I had no idea what more I could do.

***

A poll by JL Partners suggested that Labour's lead over the Conservatives had fallen to just 12 points.

Despite the DWP, of which he was minister, handing out benefits that they shouldn't have done on an astronomical scale as though they were confetti, Mel Stride branded

Starmer as “No idea Keir”, which was both true yet at the same time rather hypocritical.

Sunak and Starmer agreed to appear in an ITV-hosted TV debate at a time when several more MPs announced they were standing down.

The socialist ideological dream (better described as an illogical nightmare) that defines the Labour Party had been an anathema to me ever since I studied Politics for one of my A-levels at school. There I had been taught and subsequently learnt the truth of as a taxpayer that socialism ultimately fails because government cannot give anything to anybody that they don’t first take away from somebody else, nor can they multiply wealth by dividing it.

The Labour Party has never understood that the country’s economy is an ecosystem whereby if you destroy one part of it, you risk upsetting another, and therefore unsettle the whole balance. As the late, great PM Baroness Margaret Thatcher succinctly put it, “The problem with socialism is that you eventually run out of other people’s money.” One doesn’t need to be a rocket scientist to work out that it’s not possible to legislate the poor into prosperity by legislating the wealthy out of prosperity.

Motoring journalist and farmer Jeremy Clarkson made the same point although less eloquently when he articulated the injustice: “What I hate most about Labour is they believe that if you work hard all your life and make some savings to tide you over in your old age, those savings are theirs. And that they should be given to people who haven't worked at all." His comments brought to mind the same sense of contradiction that I felt whenever I used to see the *'Socialist Worker'* newspaper on sale.

In the distorted fantasy world in which they live and preach, it's apparently wrong to make more money than someone else, and those that are successful should be brought down to the same level as the hard-done-by and the idle, through ever more punitive taxation. They chose to ignore the fact that high earners not only spend their money but also pay a huge amount in taxes as well as employing many other people.

Labour stated their intent to add VAT to private school fees, which represented a double hit to aspiration, was economically unsound, and vindictive in the way it punished those who had the temerity to earn enough and/or scrimp and save to pay for the privilege when logic would suggest that they should actually be offered tax credits for freeing up spaces in the state sector for which they were already paying.

In the real world, however, people should aspire and be encouraged to create wealth and pay their dues in taxes, which will then benefit the economy and others less fortunate than themselves. So, like them or loathe them, the rich do redistribute their wealth by spending a lot of it, which in turn keeps a lot of people in jobs. Churchill had got it right when he said: "For a nation to try to tax itself into prosperity is like a man standing in a bucket and trying to lift himself up by the handle."

Despite his record as a European human rights lawyer who had championed an open border policy I'd actually been strangely relieved and even a little optimistic when Starmer became leader of the Labour Party in 2020, as I reasoned that no one could be worse than his predecessor, the insidious, unkempt, and dangerously far-left-wing socialist Jeremy Corbyn[17] who'd had an increasingly small cult-like following. Any government should have credible and strong opposition to hold them to account and keep them in check, and the equally disheveled former PM Boris Johnson needed that more than most, He had characteristics that were a cross between a shopping trolley and a badly behaved, over-enthusiastic Labrador that needed keeping under control and his party had only itself to blame for failing to do so.

---

[17] *Jeremy Corbyn: Following Ed Miliband's resignation after the Labour party lost the election, he won the subsequent leadership election to succeed him. Having been a member of the _ Party_ since 1965, he has served as MP for Islington North since 1983 until his expulsion from the party in 2024.He is now an independent,*

If former Conservative PM John Major had been caricatured in ITV's *Spitting Image* puppet show as being 'grey' in colour, then the dull and robotic Starmer could be better described as lacking in any colour at all, except perhaps beige. He didn't display an ounce of charisma and everything he said was delivered in his trademark adenoidal voice, but I hoped that he would at the very least do a better job than the feeble Jeremy Corbyn - which shouldn't have been too difficult - but he never managed to.

Whilst he presented better than the unkempt Corbyn, who never looked entirely comfortable in a jacket and tie, Starmer came across rather like a mortgage advisor from Swindon, and the sort of person you'd want to avoid sitting next to at the Christmas party. Even in the weekly televised pantomime-like "Punch and Judy" show which masquerades as PM Questions, he had been disappointing from the start of his tenure, and both he and his party had proved to be absolutely hopeless, inept and ineffectual in opposition. He had displayed bewildering levels of prevarication for several years, so why anyone would believe that he or his party would perform any better in government was quite beyond me.

Wednesday 29th May

Front pages:

Daily Mirror: COPS DROP RAYNER PROBE

Daily Telegraph: Sunak: I'm talking to Johnson about the election

i: Triple lock plus to save retirees 28p a week on state pension

Metro: TAX BATTLE RAGES OVER PENSIONS

Sean Lever texted to say that the candidates' team in Central Office had finally acknowledged receipt of my application, which was now in the process of being vetted, so this was at least a sign of some progress. He also said that the decision was imminent with regard to standing in the Daventry constituency, so I spent what would turn out to be a wasted morning researching and mugging up on this ordinary town and its outlying villages.

***

At the start of what appeared to be, and would turn out to be, his 'farewell tour', Rishi Sunak was asked whether he was concerned about the polls and, in a burst of irrational bravado, the PM said he wasn't. Polls are as notoriously inaccurate as the weather forecasts that had caught him out on the doorstep of 'Number 10' the previous week, but he should have been extremely worried, and his bluff didn't convince anyone to the contrary. He was also photographed posing with a pint of beer like a naughty schoolboy, which was an uncomfortable image as he was well known to be a teetotaller who doesn't even like the taste of alcohol-free beer.

Of more significance was his rejection of the idea of a deal with Nigel Farage, who had suggested they should "have a conversation", despite the fact that in 2019 NF had stood down some of his Brexit Party candidates in marginal seats, thus handing a huge boost to Boris Johnson's prospects.

At this stage, Reform was polling at about 12%, with most of its support coming from disaffected Conservative voters "of a certain age" like me.

The British Medical Association (BMA) announced that junior doctors would stage a five-day strike in the days immediately ahead of polling day, the timing of which Sunak described as incredibly cynical.

Thursday 30th May

Front pages:

The Times: Back me for low interest rates, Sunak tells voters

Daily Express: YOU'VE BUCKLED! HUNT'S WIN AS LABOUR BACKS DOWN ON TAX RISES

Daily Mirror: We're behind you, Keir

Metro: 'CYNICAL' ELECTION DOC STRIKE

NF appeared on BBC TV's *Question Time* programme and pointed out that the election campaign to date had been so boring that Lord Lucan [18]was back on the front page of the *Daily Mail.*

He also reiterated that, had he been given a six-month run at it, he had intended to stand for election, but that with only six weeks it was an impossible task and that he would not be doing so - which didn't fill me with confidence as a PPC who would have even less time to campaign. Much less time, as it turned out.

Starmer denied blocking left-wing candidates, as veteran Labour politician Diane Abbott accused her party of carrying out a "cull". Although she had been reinstated as an MP after a long suspension, she was still barred from standing in the GE.

A boost for Labour came when Mark Logan, former PPS and Conservative MP for Bolton North East, announced he was standing down from Parliament and would be

---

[18] *Lord Lucan was* ***a*** *British peer and gambler who vanished in 1974 after being suspected of killing his children's nanny and attempting to murder his wife. Despite never being tracked down, an inquest jury declared him to be the nanny's killer in 1975.*

transferring his allegiance and voting for Labour at the election. He cited ideological differences with his former party, saying that it was now “unrecognisable”, which resonated with the views of many of the party faithful.

Friday 31st May

Front pages:

Daily Express: EXPOSED! SPLITS IN LABOUR RANKS

The Guardian: Pressure on Starmer to end ‘purge of Labour left’

i: Boost for Tories as Reform UK slips in polls but Labour still far ahead

Financial Times: Voters brace for tax increases despite assurances from Labour and Tories

My girlfriend and I went to see my local rugby team, the Northampton Saints, play at home. Friday evening matches at Franklin’s Gardens are always popular and great fun, and helped by their victory over Saracens, this was no exception - especially as it guaranteed them a place in the final at Twickenham (now incongruously named after a German insurance company).

What made it an even more enjoyable evening was that my fellow season ticket holders and other friends were surprisingly supportive of the idea of me possibly standing for Reform, even though I still hadn't actually been allocated a seat to contest at that point.

***

Former US President Donald Trump was found guilty on all counts in a historic criminal trial in New York, thus becoming the first former or serving president to be convicted of a crime. He was in the midst of making a bid to return to the White House when he was found guilty on 34 counts of falsifying business records and breaking election law, which included concealing a payment to buy the silence of former porn star Stormy Daniels.

It had been common knowledge that Nigel Farage was a longstanding friend and ally of his US counterpart and had long stated his intention to help him win the 2024 Presidential election in November. Their relationship was well chronicled but, as with vice president-in-waiting JD Vance, it was neither new nor manufactured, as they had known each other for twenty years and shared similar ideologies and a genuine meeting of minds.

Those who don't like either of them are often the same people who dislike tabloid newspapers, brash political broadcasts or hearing the truth because they are forthright, brazen and in your face. The conceited and tangerine-coloured Trump is as erratic and unpredictable as the British weather and regularly articulates his controversial opinions in an unsophisticated, comedic and childlike manner. He has such an enormously overinflated ego that, when he tweeted "Long live the King", most of his followers assumed he was actually referring to himself rather than King Charles.

A journalist friend of mine had pointed out that the mistake people tend to make with the inconsistent and unpredictable Donald Trump is to take him literally but not seriously, when in fact exactly the opposite approach is required.

Farage had only recently told *The Daily Telegraph* that he had huge regrets about not standing, and the news of the court verdict may have been the catalyst which changed his mind.

Saturday 1st June

Front pages:

i weekend: UK voters' message to the Tories: it's time for change

The Times: Starmer: I'll create wealth

We entertained (or at least I hope we did...) a few people for dinner that evening, at which I confided in a good friend, Hugo Brown - a former Tory councillor and Constituency Chairman - that I was thinking of standing for Reform UK.

I have to admit to being unnaturally and, as it transpired, unnecessarily cautious about telling him. Even though differences in political opinions shouldn't come between friends, I was acutely aware of how divisive the subject of politics can be and had no wish to compromise relationships. Although it had been a boozy evening amongst convivial company, it still took me until the end of the evening to pluck up sufficient 'Dutch Courage' to mention it to him, especially as he doesn't drink wine and stuck to non-alcoholic gin and tonics all evening, so was likely to be far sharper and more rational than I was by that stage.

Despite expecting to receive a frosty reception, it was the opposite. He endorsed my decision to stand up for my beliefs and do something about it, even if it was in opposition to the party that we had both voted for all our lives. He was remarkably encouraging, which was a welcome relief, and assured me that he wasn't just being polite to me as his host.

***

Of particular resonance to me and the other PPCs in Northamptonshire, NF told voters in the East Midlands that voting Reform would "affect who Labour's opposition will be."

Sunday 2nd June

Front pages:

Sunday People: I taught Rishi but I'd never vote for him

Sunday Express: LABOUR'S £1,000 'TAX RAID' ON OAPs

The Sunday Times: Labour offers MPs peerages to step down

The Sunday Telegraph: Labour will betray pensioners again, says Chancellor

The Observer: Sunak suffers poll blow as cash-for-votes row erupts

The Mail on Sunday: TORIES' S.O.S. TO RISHI: GIVE US TAX CUTS NOW

Drinks with Simon and Lucy Hill, who were old friends of Richard's, but by this time he was far too busy campaigning to take time out to be socialising. Although his lovely ex-wife Emma was there, I decided it might be appropriate to avoid her, just in case there was any conflict of interest.

In the meantime, I had messaged Richard to say that I'd now been told by Sean Lever that the aforementioned Daventry was no longer an option, as the Candidates Team had (again, quite correctly in my opinion) decided that the incumbent there, Scott Cameron, was actually doing a really good job (as he would prove come 4th July).

As a result, I was asked by Sean to consider standing in Kettering, where the PPC had decided to stand down due to the demands of his job in the NHS.

By this stage, I felt that this was all becoming a bit nonsensical and far too last-minute. With the election now only just over four weeks away, it was cutting it fine to say the least, especially as official nominations were due to be lodged by all parties with the local council's electoral offices by the following Friday.

Richard's response was once again ever optimistic and encouraging; his assurance seemed almost cavalier as he insisted there was "plenty of time"! On the basis that I had still not received any confirmation from the external screening company that I had passed - whatever the vetting process actually entailed - I didn't share his confidence. There was no sense of feeling from any other sources that my application was being taken very seriously by anyone else involved in the process.

I was already aware of the hideous mistake the party had made earlier in the year when it rebuked one of their candidates, Tommy Cawkwell [19] and then sacked him for being inactive, although it emerged that he had died. At the time they remarked "We can't afford to have people doing nothing in an election year". When they discovered the error a party spokesman compounded it with his insensitive choice of words by saying that they were "mortified" Needless to say this didn't exactly fill me with confidence about their processes and powers of communication.

At this point, I was ready to put all my frustrations down to experience and write the whole idea off, so I went to bed that evening trying to think of anything I knew about Kettering which, other than the fact that it was quite a long way to get to from where I live, wasn't a great deal, so it didn't keep me awake for too long.

***

Whether it was coincidental or not, once 'The Donald' had been found guilty, Nigel did what all seasoned politicians are so good at and executed a spectacular and surprising U-turn, the likes of which any self-respecting rally driver would be proud of.

---

[19] *Tommy Cawkwell, an RNLI volunteer, was the York Central candidate for Reform UK who failed to respond to a number of phone calls and emails from the party who rescinded his candidacy without knowing that he had died following the selection process.*

Only days after ruling out the possibility, he confirmed that he would not only be taking over from Richard Tice as leader of Reform UK for the next five years, but also announced that he would make a return to front-line politics and be standing for election after all. With only 31 days to go until the election and despite seven previous failures to win a seat in the Commons, he would once again try to break his duck by taking on the Tory-held seat in Clacton-on-Sea in Essex.

Monday 3rd June

Front pages:

i: Labour plan for softer Brexit deal too ambitious, EU insiders warn

What would turn out to be a busy week started with me texting Sean, asking if he'd had any news about my candidacy. Predictably, he hadn't, but asked me if I was absolutely sure that I would stand for Kettering in North Northamptonshire.

Although it wasn't my first (or even my second...) choice, perversely the frustrations that I'd experienced with the lack of progress so far had made me even more determined to get involved and stand up for what I believed in, so it was very much a case of third time lucky. The distance from home would make things logistically even more difficult than Daventry would have done, but at least it was still the same county.

I later learnt that one of my party colleagues was the candidate for Swansea West, despite living in Kent, which required interminable hours braving the delights of the M4, and that made me count my lucky stars and feel relatively fortunate that however much time I had to spend on the campaign trail, at least I'd be able to sleep in my own bed at night.

Researching Kettering didn't take much time, as there was not very much to distinguish it. The constituency comprised a largely unremarkable Midlands market town surrounded by a variety of pleasant villages, interspersed with housing conurbations and industrial estates, which included the homes of well-known British brands like Weetabix and Timpsons.

Like many towns in the county, it had a longstanding historical association with the leather and shoe-making industries, although this was now largely limited to Cheaney Shoes, owned by Jonathan and William Church, scions of the eponymous shoe manufacturer which is now owned by an Italian company.

My first ever holiday job had been in Northampton when I was working as a gofer for an F1 racing team before I started racing myself, and I was proud to have subsequently owned a house in the county for more than thirty years. It has always been known as the county of “Spires and Squires” and has a greater concentration of stately homes than any other county - but I didn’t come across many of either in the constituency which was destined to become my ‘second home’ for the next few weeks.

I was hard pushed to find out much more of any interest, other than the fact that my ‘patch’ was home to Wicksteed theme park, which I’d never heard of but which dates back to 1921 and is one of the oldest of its kind in the UK. I concluded that unless you were specifically visiting an attraction like this, or actually lived there, Kettering was probably a part of the country you were more likely to drive through en route to somewhere else without stopping for anything other than fuel or sustenance. It wasn’t a town that I’d ever had cause to visit, although, having competed at the nearby - and since abandoned - race circuit at Rockingham a few times, at least I had travelled through the constituency on occasion.

However, before I first ventured there, I did read that a survey from a couple of years ago found that the town itself was voted the happiest place in Northamptonshire to live. As I was to discover over the course of the next few weeks of campaigning, that was reflected in the almost unanimously sunny disposition of the people I met and spoke to, including the many who were clearly not going to put an X against my name in the election. After all, it's the people that make the community, for better or worse, and I rarely felt anything other than welcomed, even though I was obviously a complete stranger to everyone I met.

***

Sunak suffered the latest blunder in his campaign so far when a video of his party's first election broadcast was released showing the Union Jack flying upside down. To deliberately do this is a signal indicating distress, and if that was the intention, then it worked well.[20]

Apart from the very real prospect of NF winning the seat in Clacton, his presence immediately added huge momentum to the efforts of the other PPCs and colleagues in the Reform party, injecting renewed vigour into their efforts.

However, this was also hugely damaging to the Conservatives and represented Rishi's worst nightmare. His gambol had backfired, and not only did it pose an immediate concern for the incumbent Tory candidate in Clacton, but the presence of the former UKIP and Brexit Party leader also

---

[20] *Flying or displaying the Union Jack upside down is also known as "lese Majeste" which means insulting the Crown and is theoretically still a crime in the UK and commonwealth!*

dramatically increased the likelihood of wooing right-leaning votes from Conservatives and put Reform in a position to antagonise the Tories in their post-election in-house squabbling.

Sunak was right to be in fear of Farage and his destructive potential and he will have understood that the process of Brexit had broken his party. Within it, many went into meltdown and were already in disagreement as to whether Reform should team up with them, with several of their MPs openly pleading with Nigel not to split the vote.

Tuesday 4th June

Front pages:

The Times: Farage's return and new poll deal to Sunak

The Guardian: Tory alarm as Farage takes control of Reform UK

i: Farage blows apart Tory election plan with surprise challenge to Sunak

Daily Mail: RISHI'S DARKEST HOUR

Daily Mirror: SUNAK'S ELECTION CRISIS

Daily Express: VOTE FOR FARAGE IS MORE LIKELY TO END UP WITH STARMER IN NO 10

The Independent: Farage election shock: I will stand as an MP and leader of Reform

Financial Times: Twin blow to Tories as Farage enters the fray and polls predict a drubbing

The Daily Telegraph: I'm back to lead the revolt

Metro: TORIES FACE A RECORD ROUT

My day had begun with an email from the Head of Electoral Services in Kettering outlining the arrangements for the delivery of the UKPGE (UK Parliamentary General Election). This was both intriguing and encouraging as it indicated that they knew something that I didn't regarding my standing as a candidate, because I still hadn't had any formal notification from the party itself.

Sean messaged me to say that, once again, he'd been chasing up my candidacy to no avail but also to ask me yet again if I was definitely prepared to stand in Kettering. Whilst I was happy to again confirm that I was willing to, I certainly wasn't prepared in any way for what was to follow. By now he'd asked me the question so many times that I was almost suspicious about what I was letting myself in for. In any case, with little over a month to go until the election, I'd become rather despondent about my prospects and questioned what little chance I had left to campaign within such a short timeframe – which would be a maximum of 30 days if I was lucky.

Two hours after the correspondence from Electoral Services, I finally received an acknowledgement from 'The Candidates Team' at Reform telling me that they had received my application to stand as a PPC, and that, almost three weeks after I had submitted it, I had passed the initial (as it turned out, non-existent) vetting stage. This process is likely to have been more thorough had I applied for a job at my local petrol station and supposedly included various background checks which would continue up to the point at which they provided me with a certificate of authorisation to stand. I'm not sure how important it was, but it would have been nice to have had it, if only to mark the occasion and hang it alongside the repetitive pictures of racing cars on the wall of my office, although it didn't surprise me that I never actually received it.

The email also reminded me that it was my responsibility to ensure that my "social media presence was appropriate for somebody wishing to run for high office", something that was going to be very strongly endorsed by my elder son.

By now, I'd had a lot of dialogue with Sean in his capacity as gatekeeper and county coordinator, but I hadn't actually met him. Together with his wife Lisa, we finally did so that evening, and it was good to finally put a face to the name. We arranged to meet on the outskirts of Northampton at the functional but insalubrious 'Holiday Inn' hotel, which struck me as a misleading name because, like Kettering, the drab and mundane Midlands town is not most people's idea of a holiday destination. I assumed that our meeting might have been part of the vetting and/or interview process but, if it was, I assumed that I'd passed it.

Neither of us knew it at the time, but within a few days, Sean was destined to become my agent, though by default rather than design. He commended me on deciding to stand for election and pointed out that it is not an easy decision and required bravery, conviction and hard work. He was helpful in describing the process and bureaucracy involved in morphing from being a PPC into a Parliamentary Candidate (PC), but wasn't in a position to provide me with much advice or guidance about structuring a campaign - which was no criticism of him and although a surprise, it was exciting and worrying in equal measure.

I naively thought that I might be provided with some sort of instruction manual or written notes directing me as to what was required and expected of me and how to go about it, but I left the meeting none the wiser, and with nothing by way of promotional materials or handouts other than a clutch of decidedly 'pre-loved' looking but still quite smart, light blue party rosettes. As it turned out, they were the only things the party were able to provide me by way of material support. Apart from Sean's thanks and encouragement, I returned home unsure as to exactly what I'd let myself in for, blissfully unaware of how to go about things and wondering if I had been gifted a poisoned chalice and if, rather than being gently 'parachuted' into the constituency, I'd actually just been dropped from a great height, unarmed and ill-prepared, into the mire!

By the time I got back home and in front of my screens, Sean had already added me to the WhatsApp group that he'd set up, which would now link him and our group of seven Northamptonshire PPCs together for the duration of our respective campaigns. As the others were all weeks ahead of me in the process, this was something of a lifesaver, as I was able to absorb and learn from their posts about what they were doing and experiencing, although it was clearly very much a case of the blind leading the blind!

Membership of this exclusive 'club' was to be one of the few resources that I had to draw on, and what I learnt from it was by way of osmosis, imitation and process of elimination. Although it was naturally each man (there were no female candidates in our domain, and far too few standing for Reform nationwide) for himself to an extent, everyone was very helpful in terms of sharing and swapping information and their day-to-day experiences, and we all learnt from each other to varying degrees. I was very grateful for this, as it also provided some much-needed levity over the next month or so, and a platform through which Sean could, if not guide, cajole and encourage us as and when appropriate.

Sean's introduction to the group had led to warm messages of welcome from the other Northamptonshire PCs which, thanks to the wonders of predictive texting, were variously addressed to me as Crispian Esley, Christian, Crispin Beazly, and even Cristiano - which sounded more exotic - but I'm very used to that and have been called far worse over the years, as will have anyone lumbered with a mildly awkward and clumsy-sounding name like mine. The important thing was that it immediately created a camaraderie between us and whilst we would all be fighting for our own individual seats, there was a sense of us all being in this together and not alone.

Sean had explained that the first thing to do, and of top priority, was to obtain the requisite number of ten signatures to support my nomination. This was easier said than done, as I literally didn't know a soul in the town of Kettering or any of the outlying villages and communities, and whilst a database of members and supporters existed, the catch-22 was that I quite rightly didn't have access to it at this stage.

Sean came to the rescue by circulating an email overnight, asking for supporters on the constituency database who might be prepared to add their signatures to support my candidacy. He was allowed to provide them with my personal email address so that any replies would be directed back to me. By 9.00 am the next morning, I was very relieved that his entreaties had elicited sufficient response from enough kind people who agreed to do so.

***

Nigel's change of mind and his surprise challenge was a bombshell for Sunak and had made the front pages of almost every newspaper, as he was quoted as saying that he was "back to lead the revolt", leading to headlines suggesting that this was Rishi's "darkest hour" and predicting the Tories were facing a record rout.

Within 24 hours of appointing himself party leader and declaring his intention to stand for Parliament, NF arrived in the seaside town of Clacton with an event on the pier that was attended by hundreds of people.

"What do I have to offer you?" he asked the assembled throng. "Well, I can promise you that I do know one thing. That a woman can't have a penis! You won't get any woke PC nonsense from me!" It may have been a random and out-of-context comment, but it was still met with enthusiastic applause from the crowd as he demonstrated his instinctive feel for public opinion, so rare in most politicians, and went on to plead, "send me to Parliament to be a bloody nuisance!"

His visit predictably included taking in a pint at the local Wetherspoons pub, 'The Moon and Starfish', but as he left it, a disaffected bystander soaked him by throwing a milkshake over him - a repeat of his 2019 campaign trail when a Geordie threw a banana and caramel version over him in Newcastle, an act which led to "milkshaking" - the act of dousing public figures with the drink - being officially recognised as a word by the Collins Dictionary later that year.

As of today, encouraged by the news of Farage's surprise return to lead the party and contest the seat in Clacton, party membership had now surged to 45,000.

Wednesday 5th June

Front pages:

The Daily Telegraph: Starmer on the ropes over tax

Daily Express: KAPOW! RISHI FLOORS STARMER OVER £2,000 TAX RISE

The Times: Labour accused on tax as Sunak comes out fighting

The Guardian: Leaders clash on migration, tax and NHS in ill-tempered debate

i: 2024 election ignites during angry TV clash

Daily Mail: Fiery Rishi comes out swinging-and lands big blows

Independent: Farage: I want to replace the Tories

Metro: SHAKY START FOR FARAGE

With the GE taking place on 4th July, what would turn out to be my one month in politics had now started, even though I still had to collate the required signatures and present them, along with other paperwork, in person by appointment to the Head of Electoral Services at the council offices before I could officially be declared a bona fide PC.

The response to Sean's email to constituency members had been remarkable, and the heartwarming willingness to help me lifted my spirits as I set about calling or emailing as many of those who'd responded as I could, booking in vague time slots to visit them.

This was easier said than done; 'my' designated constituency may have been in the same county that I lived in, but it was the best part of an hour's drive to an area that I barely knew. My notoriously bad sense of direction didn't help, but even allowing for the fact that I didn't know the geography of the constituency, I was obliged to fit my schedule around those of the kind strangers who had agreed to act as signatories for me.

Although I only needed a proposer, seconder and eight other signatures, Sean had warned me that they all needed to be on both the electoral roll as well as residing within the, recently redefined, boundaries of the constituency. Their details and signatures all needed to be on the same page because, had just one of them not met those criteria, the whole document would be invalid and not accepted by the Electoral Services team.

As an insurance policy, I decided to collect a few more, in the vain hope that it would add to my chances of being accepted as a parliamentary candidate and, unnecessarily as it turned out, actually collected seventeen.

Of course, none of those who'd agreed to add their respective names knew anything about me, as my details hadn't yet been posted on the party's website, so each and every one of my meetings almost took the form of informal 'interviews', rather than take the form of "door stepping", the delights and challenges of which I was yet to experience.

Understandably, those I met wanted to know where this 'newbie' with a slightly odd name, who was going to represent them, had come from and to establish his credentials for the role they were going to entrust me with.

Most important was that they wanted to know I was genuine-or "authentic", in the modern vernacular-and that my views aligned with theirs. Each meeting involved me being invited into their homes for cups of tea, and most required at least half an hour of my time, which made for a very long first day on the job.

Everyone I met that day was, of course, a member of Reform UK and thanked me for putting my head above the parapet on behalf of the party and Nigel (they all seemed to affectionately refer to him by his Christian name, which I thought a bit overfamiliar), who some likened to putting a fox into a hen house.

All of the meetings were enjoyable and interesting, giving me insight into both the local concerns and national issues that were on people's minds, and a taste of what to expect when talking to less enthusiastic constituents.

Even after my first day in Kettering, I had some sympathy with NF's rather tactless remarks to his constituents that one of the drawbacks of standing for Parliament was that he did not want "to spend every Friday for the next five years in Clacton". I might have felt the same, but I was very wary of expressing similar views in Kettering, knowing that doing so might bite me in the backside and would be unlikely to do me any favours come polling day.

En route to Kettering, I was amused to receive a call from a rather concerned Sean to ask if I'd ever previously stood for Parliament, as there was a rumour circulating from local Tory representatives that a former Conservative MP was standing for Reform UK. I assured him that I hadn't, and that the rumour mills may have got their wires crossed, confusing me with Crispin Blunt, the controversial former Tory MP for Reigate, who had previously announced that he would be standing down as an independent MP and not contesting the 2024 General Election. We shared the same initials, a very similar first name, and coincidentally had both attended Wellington College at the same time, but I'd never met him. So if they weren't guilty of deliberately trying to stir things up, it's likely someone had simply put two and two together and made five.

Whilst every political party had been wrong-footed by the PM's early announcement of a snap election, they all had well-funded and long-established infrastructures which had been working towards the 2024 election for the last eighteen months. Unlike them, however, Reform was so new that it had not had the time to set up a formal structure, and its operations were at times amateur at best and often chaotic and unprofessional, as they would admit and start to address after the election.

The first of what would be many experiences of the lack of coordination was that, whilst still on the road zig-zagging across my new 'territory' at 6.40 that evening, I received an email congratulating me on having successfully completed the "candidate assessment process". I never discovered what that had entailed but it certainly hadn't involved me directly in any way. It also confirmed that my application had been "fast-tracked" (a misnomer if ever there was one) thus offering me the opportunity to be the Reform UK PPC in Kettering. Having been used to both an industry and a sport in which things move with great speed, nothing in the process so far could be described as 'fast' in any way, but again, this was a function of a severe lack of resources and manpower.

The email also asked me to sign and return an NDA, which I had already done the previous week, and promised me a "Training and Assessment Day", which I would very much have welcomed but, somewhat predictably, I never heard any more about!

Of far greater immediate importance was the instruction to attend an online GDPR (General Data Protection Regulation) briefing for candidates at 7.00 pm that evening. This was the latest hurdle I had to navigate and, as I was to learn, of critical importance. Without completing it, I'd find my hands tied behind my back, as I wouldn't be given access to the in-house database or, more crucially, my Reform UK email account for Kettering-which was an essential tool-nor would I be on the circulation list for briefings or press releases.

Twenty minutes' warning was quite ridiculous and unrealistically short notice, and like everything else in this process, seemed thoroughly disorganised and chaotic. I would, of course, have attended if I'd been able to, but it just wasn't possible as I was still on the road dashing around the county gaining the requisite supporting signatures and being 'interrogated' by my signatories, which was necessarily time-consuming.

Ahead of Friday's deadline and my meeting at the Electoral offices, this had to be my top priority, and I didn't return home until after 10.30 pm, exhausted after a long, challenging but ultimately fruitful day.

I reported back to Sean that, despite it being more than required, I had amassed 17 signatures, and he congratulated me for going from nothing to a PPC in less than 24 hours and advised me to pour myself a drink.

***

In their first televised debate, Keir Starmer declared that Sunak had his "back against the wall" and had resorted to lies.

In the meantime, our leader was quoted as saying that it had been "quite frightening" when he'd been attacked and had a banana milkshake thrown over him the previous day, when he started his first day of campaigning as the party's

PC in Clacton. The incident certainly brought into focus the security aspect of campaigning. The 25-year-old perpetrator, who was swiftly arrested on suspicion of assault, had thrown the drink in his face before throwing the McDonald's cup at him-but of course, the contents could have been any number of more harmful substances.

They say there's no such thing as bad publicity, and history will never relate whether the incident had any impact on sales at the fast food chain.

Whether the stunt helped Reform was also debatable, but a furious Richard Tice said, "The juvenile moron who threw a drink over Nigel has just gained us hundreds of thousands more votes. We will not be bullied or put off the campaign trail." Whatever the truth, the latest nationwide opinion poll now put us just two points behind the Tories on 17%, and the incident might have been partially responsible for that.

The Guardian was unflattering in its commentary of Nigel's first day of campaigning, suggesting that his speeches were a familiar narrative: "It is the dish cooked up for Brexit, now back on the menu under the Reform UK brand," but that they were "satisfying a national appetite".

Thursday 6th June

Front pages:

The Guardian: Sunak lied to country over Labour tax and spend plans, says Starmer

The Daily Telegraph: Hunt issues challenge to Starmer over taxes on property

The Independent: Treasury trashes Rishi Sunak over Labour tax claim

Financial Times: Starmer accuses Sunak of 'resorting to lies' over Labour £2,000 tax rise claim

I received yet another request for the signed NDA form, which I patiently completed and returned for a third time. Thirty years spent working in the City and my subsequent career had taught me enough about the vagaries and requirements of GDPR, and the need for compliance. Recognising the importance of completing the course, I had emailed the party as soon as I woke at 5.30 am, explaining the situation and offering to take part in an online session at any time, day or night, so that I could get my campaign moving forward as soon as possible.

As was becoming familiar practice I didn't receive a response for several more days, so it didn't seem as though the party shared my sense of urgency.

I received another message welcoming me as a candidate, this time from the somewhat eccentric but friendly and very effective Gawain Towler, who was the National Press Officer. A colourful character who, when explaining the party leader's appeal, had once told a political website that "Nigel Farage has this unerring ability to touch the clitoris of public opinion." In one of the few communications I received from him, he suggested that the process was going to be a fun and wild ride, which he likened to "white water rafting with the press taking up the role of the spume around me" which I learnt was rather more poetic than reality!

He explained that he was being inundated with local media requests and was in the invidious position that if PCs didn't respond to their requests, the journalists would get onto him, and that, with the best will in the world, he wouldn't have the time to respond to each and every one of them. He stressed the importance of responding to these via the constituency email address, which I was still a very long way from having access to.

This was another example of the dire shortage of human capital, in that he too was operating as a one-man band. Gawain asked for understanding that, as he was working alone, he was likely to take a little time getting back to me - which, as things transpired, was an understatement. Farage re-entering the fray had changed everything for the better from the party's perspective, but had also upped the workload, tempo and ante in every respect.

Gawain also asked for a 600-word article explaining why I was standing, together with a short bio, which I duly delivered. He also needed some photos of me "looking human", but I chose to send him those that my younger son had taken on his phone, with me in a suit jacket which was now far too large for me and, as with all those which were used, had my head tilted to the point that it made me look like I only had one ear.

I've always recognised that I had a good face for radio and never considered myself especially photogenic at the best of times, but "human" I did not look, and this was on a new level - to the extent that, in the unlikely event that Madame Tussaud's waxworks museum ever wanted to create an effigy of my likeness, it would surely have taken pole position in their Chamber of Horrors!

I made my appointment with the Electoral Offices at Kettering Council offices for the next day, at which I would complete all the required paperwork, but was acutely aware that, with the time constraints, this was all cutting things very fine indeed.

That evening Juliet and I were guests at the opera at Garsington, where I, somewhat guardedly, hinted at my intentions to my hosts, and expressed my concerns as to whether my last-minute application for candidacy would survive the bureaucratic process. In all the excitement of catching up with our friends, I had made the "beginner's mistake" of forgetting to turn off my mobile phone and was receiving constant messages and missed urgent calls from Sean Lever and several others.

Fortunately, there was no mobile reception at Garsington, because it would not have been popular with either my hosts or the rest of the audience to have had the performance interrupted by my ringtone - which was the sound of barking dogs. In retrospect, although it would have been heresy to some people to have the performance interrupted by the intermittent sounds of dogs woofing, it would probably have fitted in with, and even enhanced, the performance, which in this case was a thoroughly modern interpretation of *Platée*. In retrospect I could probably have got away with the indiscretion of leaving the wretched thing switched on and gone unnoticed after all.

***

The latest YouGov poll now showed Reform just two points behind the Tories; Labour led with 40%, followed by Conservatives with 19% and Reform with 17%.

Whilst I was enjoying the opera with Juliet and our friends in Oxfordshire, as an aspiring 'politician in waiting' over in France more than a dozen international leaders and heads of state attended major services commemorating the 80th anniversary of the D-Day landings - one of the most important events in recent history.

Farage quite justifiably criticised the PM for being staggeringly disrespectful when he literally ‘left them on the beaches’ and failed to go on to Omaha Beach in Normandy, saying, “I’ve got a country to run.” Many quipped that “Slippery Sunak” had left it a bit late to do that, but he did himself no favours when it was revealed that he’d actually left to record a TV election campaign interview that wasn’t even due to be broadcast until the following week. His failure was an almost unbelievable faux pas and led to more exasperation and disquiet in his ranks, strengthening the belief that, like his opposite number, he just wasn’t very good at politics - which is not a good look for any politician, let alone the Prime Minister.

The Spectator posed the question as to whether NF was the “meteor that will finally finish off the Tories?” Although it seemed to me that they already seemed to be doing a pretty good job of that themselves.

Friday 7th June

Front pages:

Daily Mirror: PM DITCHES D-DAY

i: Reform surges again as new polls show Farage effect

Daily Star: We agree with Nigel

Although I know a lot of people say the same, seven really is my lucky number, and I was hopeful that today's date would help things go smoothly in my quest to go one better than being a PPC and become the 7th and final Reform UK parliamentary candidate confirmed for Northamptonshire.

I was up bright and early in anticipation of my meeting at the council offices in Kettering. Sean's unwavering enthusiasm added to the excitement (of sorts...) and he generously agreed to take Friday off work so that he could accompany me to the electoral offices and help if I got into difficulty; as things turned out, I was to be extremely grateful for his presence, which was a lifesaver.

Our allocated slot to meet with Electoral Services was at midday, and I made a point of getting to the anonymous and austere-looking council offices half an hour early, which was just as well, for whilst there were plenty of parking spaces, it took me twenty minutes walking between several meters and pay stations before I could find one that was in working order and could accept payment from my card. I didn't want to get off to a bad start and have my first memory of Kettering being the receipt of a parking ticket...

All candidate nominations were required to be in order and registered with the electoral office by the deadline of 4.00 pm, and my appointment at the council offices for them to go through all the necessary paperwork was at 12.00 pm. All 10 signatures had to be from people who lived within the newly defined boundaries of the constituency and who were also registered on the electoral roll and eligible to vote, which sounded straightforward enough but if either of those two parameters weren't met, the bureaucracy of the system was such that, rather than allowing candidates to use any other signatures collected on a separate sheet of paper, the council would be obliged to reject the form.

Failure, therefore, would have required the whole process to be done all over again but, as it had taken a whole day on Wednesday to collect them, and given the time constraints of the impending deadline, this would have been near impossible and my candidacy would have been refused.

Fortunately for me, Sean had taken the initiative to forward my signatures together with their addresses to the council for approval in advance, in the hope that if any of them did not meet the criteria, the Electoral Services department would let me know ahead of our meeting. It was all terribly last minute and the prospect of failing at the final post was nerve-wracking, but I was relieved to have successfully cleared this particular hurdle.

The next thing that was required was payment of the £500 deposit that each PC has to make. I had been invited to stump up for it myself, which although it hadn't occurred to me and might otherwise have come as another shock, it wasn't because by now the Reform way of going about things no longer surprised me and I was now inured to any more of them. By this time, I had jumped through so many hoops on their behalf and, as I felt that I was doing them a favour, I cheekily suggested that it might be appropriate for the party to pay this on my behalf, which I thought was the least they could do.

It was a very welcome surprise, which I wasn't prepared for, when to my amazement, thanks to Sean's entreaties they agreed to do so. It was shaping up to be my lucky day! The system of taking deposits is intended to discourage non-serious fringe candidates from taking part and wasting everyone's time, but after the election, they are returned provided that the candidate wins more than 5% of the vote in their respective constituency. As Kettering had 79,000 people on the electoral roll, this focused my mind and gave me a minimum target of winning at least 3,250 votes to focus on. I didn't want to embarrass myself, nor did I want to risk the party losing their deposit although at this stage I had no comprehension whatsoever of how many I might or should reasonably expect to win.

The fact that I didn't live in the same constituency as Kettering was an issue later raised by several voters, but it was not a problem as far as the Electoral Services team were concerned, so long as either I or my agent lived in a neighbouring one - which of course I didn't, and nor did I have an agent! Fortunately, Sean did and once again came to the rescue. In his position as DNO, he was able to step in to act in the capacity of my agent, which was not something he had bargained for particularly as he had already taken on that role for Ben Habib[21] in Wellingborough. By default, he had become my agent too, which was really generous and accommodating of him, not least because it would commit him to the responsibility for the tedious task of collating and filing all my election expenses after the event - although, in my case, these would prove to be well within the amount allowable and therefore hopefully not too onerous a job. This ensured that the final criteria were met and that I was now entitled to represent the party in my designated constituency - which was a welcome but slightly scary prospect.

---

[21] *Ben Habib is a businessman who was an MEP for London from July 2019 until the UK withdrew from the EU in January 2020.He subsequently served as a co-deputy leader of Reform UK from October 2023 to July 2024, alongside David Bull. They were both were removed from their roles and replaced by Richard Tice after the 2024 General Election.*

By the deadline, a total of 132 MPs announced they were standing down at the election, which included a record number of Conservatives. A total of 4,515 candidates were nominated, more than in any previous general election, and for better or worse, I was now one of them. My last-minute confirmation was the final piece in the Northamptonshire jigsaw and meant that not only did we collectively achieve a full house, with all 7 candidates getting their nominations accepted and over the line, but this also meant that all 47 East Midlands seats had a Reform candidate in place. The national figure for Reform UK candidates nominated was 611, plus 9 (on a joint ticket with the SDP), and this represented a 98.4% success rate - an impressive achievement.

By now, I had put a great deal of thought into standing, but this had all happened very quickly, and in the space of less than three days the reality struck home: I had gone from being a disenchanted voter to a PPC, and was now a formally approved PC whose name would be on a ballot paper for Kettering, thereby giving those who wanted it the option to vote for Reform - with my name to put an X against.

Although a highly unlikely outcome, the reality now was that if I actually won the seat and became an MP, I would be taking on the enormous and hugely important responsibility of being the elected representative of many thousands of people in the Kettering constituency. It was too late to back out now - and anyway, there was no way I was going to do that. Quite the contrary: I was now raring to get out and persuade them to actually vote for me.

Once I got back home, I read the irritating automated response to my request for an update from the NDA team, which said that once they'd filed and approved my completed NDA, they'd be able to set up my Reform email address. Contradicting themselves, they went on to say that if I'd already done this (I obviously had, otherwise I wouldn't have asked for an update...) the NDA team would "reach out to me with an update". I now had less than four weeks to go out and gather votes, and by the time I'd jumped through all the remaining hoops, I was painfully aware that I'd be left with even less than that. I felt like a dog running around in circles, chasing his own tail...

Similarly, my repeated request to attend a GDPR course as soon as possible was frustrated by the response from the candidates team, stating that although usually held on either Wednesdays or Fridays, tonight's session had been cancelled as the nomination forms were now taking priority (even though they'd expected me to drop everything on the preceding Wednesday to attend a course with just twenty minutes' notice...) and that it would be rescheduled for the next Wednesday or Friday. It wasn't - and wouldn't be until

Sunday the 16th June, leading to a further hindrance and a reduction in the precious time I had left to get my campaign rolling.

This was all becoming quite absurd because each day that passed was vital for me in the limited time available. I was infuriated to learn that the next available session would not be for another ten days, which seemed quite ridiculous - until I learned that the person leading the meeting was himself yet another candidate, and so presumably had other things to do in terms of prioritising his own campaign.

Dave Holland had emailed me yesterday asking for a smart head-and-shoulders photo ("as large as you have") and a 300-word 'bio' about what I was going to do for the residents of Kettering, which I had done immediately. However, whoever was responsible in Party HQ had still not yet got around to putting my name or details up on its website.

However, Sean had clarified the situation with the local press about Daniel Mone standing down from contesting the seat due to personal reasons, and as a result, I received a call from Sam Wildman of *The Northants Telegraph*. He asked me to send him a brief bio together with a quote as to the reasons why I had put myself forward as a candidate, and also to send a photo - which, after choosing the least unflattering one, I did. He told me he'd post something online on the newspaper's website which, given the lack of anything posted on the party's own site, I was very grateful for. He also kindly promised an interview over the course of the next few weeks, which I knew would be helpful.

I'd received a notification from someone who styled himself the Party General Manager, inviting me to a weekly Zoom call for PCs, whose mission he claimed was "to make Reform UK a year-round electioneering machine." It was a commendable statement, but I couldn't afford to wait for that to happen. The Reform party 'machine' was in desperate need of lubrication and needed to be functioning yesterday rather than tomorrow in order to get it on the road. Indeed, had the proposed "machine" been a car, it would barely have started - let alone passed its MoT test at this point...

The call began with an introduction from him which was full of good intent: "We have pockets of excellence up and down the country, but it is now time to bring that knowledge together for the benefit of all candidates, wherever they may stand." In reality, the session took the form of a welcome pep talk from Richard Tice who, before appearing on a *Radio 4* interview, had taken time off from his own campaign to express his gratitude to all those on the call - which was very welcome and much appreciated by those of us now tirelessly working on the front line.

However, the rest of it failed to deliver any details of the "mission" which might have been helpful. Despite my entreaties, I was disappointed to learn that it wasn't possible to record any of these sessions which - had they contained any relevant content - could have been extremely useful to those who'd been unable to attend. As I was always out campaigning or talking to constituents, I never managed to call in to any more of these so was never able to find out into any more of these, so was never able to find out.

Candidates had by now at least received a PDF file of a 'messaging book' which formally laid out and clarified the party's policy and agenda - soon to be formally announced by NF in the form of a 'contract'. Hopefully, this would ensure that, provided candidates stayed on message (although inevitably not all did...), we would all be singing from the same hymn sheet. Personally, I couldn't wait to get out and engage with voters.

Later that evening, after another long day, I looked forward to settling down to watch the potentially explosive BBC seven-party debate in which Farage would face off with Angela Rayner and Penny Mordaunt.

***

Predictably, the politicians clashed over the D-Day anniversary and support for war veterans, immigration, and the state of the NHS. The Conservatives were still reeling from Sunak's unforgivable blunder and darkest hour after his early disappearance from Normandy the previous day - for which he had apologised and, despite rumours to the contrary, denied that he'd ever considered missing altogether.

NF was later to accuse the PM of not believing in the country, its people, its history, or even its culture. It was left to Penny Mordaunt, then Leader of the Commons, to reply to Nigel's observation that the country had a very "unpatriotic Prime Minister" and to address the issue of his ill-advised D-Day snub, which had dominated the day's news and which she said was "completely wrong."

Once again, it was Nigel, one of the great political communicators of our time, who showed his eloquence. Being the last of the party representatives to sum up his policies, he delivered the killer blow with his pugnacious line that left his rivals reeling: "Unlike the other parties, I don't need an autocue to tell you what I believe in..." This elicited much laughter, even from a studio audience whose reactions to the politicians had suggested a heavy leaning towards the left.

In an embarrassing footnote to the day, Adam Greg, the Conservative PC for Spen Valley, withdrew his candidacy just minutes before the deadline after being confronted by the *Daily Mirror* about sharing inappropriate images of scantily clad youngsters on social media.

Saturday 8th June

Front pages:

The Independent: Tory voters want Farage to succeed Sunak as leader

Daily Mirror: SUNAK'S D-DAY SHAME

The Times: Mordaunt hits out at 'completely wrong' PM

The Guardian: Furious Tories turn on Sunak over D-Day snub

i weekend: Tories in despair as Sunak D-Day gaffe 'destroys' election hope

The Daily Telegraph: Sunak to axe stamp duty for first-time buyers

FT Weekend: Sunak accused of handing 'gift' to Reform by skipping D-Day event

As my agent, Sean was the first to receive the *Notice as to Validity of Nomination* from the very efficient head of Electoral Services, and he immediately forwarded it to me. It was a relief, and I have to admit, it stirred a modicum of pleasure.

I started my day with the realisation and the rather worrying prospect that I now had less than four weeks left to win support. I was very appreciative that, because Reform UK was a fresh new entity with great energy, this had presented a chance I wouldn't have had with any of the other major parties, who had an established infrastructure and process. Unless I had stood as an independent-which was of absolutely no interest to me-there would have been no opportunity like this. I was not only aware of the incredible chance the party had given me but also of the enormous responsibility that came with it.

First, however, I was entered to compete in an event for historic racing cars at the East Midlands circuit, Donington Park. This provided me with my first opportunity to test the temperature with people and gauge a wider cross-section of public opinion.

Word had spread quickly amongst my racing friends and contemporaries, many of whom had travelled from different parts of the country. They came from a variety of age groups, social demographics, and political leanings. Even though I wouldn't have been allowed to attach my recently acquired Reform rosettes to my bright red race suit (the colours would have clashed anyway...), a surprising number of people approached me to talk about the party. With only one exception, I was encouraged to find their reactions uniformly positive-and they weren't just being polite. Unfortunately, none of them came from my own newly allocated constituency but they had provided a useful sounding board.

Candidates were already asking amongst themselves not *if* they could bet on themselves, but *where* they could. I wasn't prepared to be drawn into the dialogue because, intuitively, the idea didn't feel right, I would have felt conflicted in doing so. In any case thanks to the conspicuously blank pages on the party website, there wasn't a lot of relevant information about me available for the bookies to set odds on.

I'm not a betting man anyway, but if I *was* going to bet on anyone, the last person it would be on is me-if for no other reason than not to jinx myself..! What other people chose to do with their own money was up to them, but odds at the bookies showed that a lot of bets were being placed on Reform UK which indicated the momentum the party was gaining. Within the gambling community, anyway...!

***

From the reactions of the biased left-wing studio audience chosen by the BBC for the previous evening's seven-party debate, one might have assumed the opposite. However, a poll of TV viewers reported by *The Daily Telegraph* told a very different story, putting the Reform leader way ahead as the clear winner, with over 58% approval compared to second-placed Penny Mordaunt on 17%, and Labour's Angela Rayner flopping completely on 10%.

The PM's D-Day gaffe had made people *really* angry, and his announcement that he had cancelled all media interviews for the day only compounded the outrage. However, it did inspire the *Matt* cartoon in *The Daily Telegraph*, which referred to the faux pas by portraying two youths walking down the street, with one remarking to the other: "If Rishi Sunak says I have to do National Service, I'll say I have an important TV interview to do." It had also led to some levity amongst candidates, who jokingly asked whether the PM had cancelled his interviews because he had a "Remembrance event" to attend..!

Another error for the beleaguered Conservative Party came in what was labeled a *'Special Edition'*-no less-of their broadsheet handout/leaflet *Your Future*, which was printed in their traditional and striking colour of... erm, red..! Meanwhile, in my own constituency, they were apparently putting them out in green, which was as crazy as the idea of the Green Party printing *their* leaflets in red!

There must have been some method in their confused madness somewhere, but it seemed as though they were going out of their way *not* to win. If it was part of a strategy, it was one I couldn't fathom and it also suggested that, despite their far greater resources than us, they were just as uncoordinated as we were in so many respects. At least, as the underfunded new kids on the block, Reform UK had an excuse!

Sunday 9th June

Front pages:

Sunday Times: Starmer's 'triple lock' pledge on not taxing tax

Sunday Telegraph: Starmer's net zero plans 'risk blackouts'

Sunday Express: FARAGE: WE'RE NOW 'REAL' OPPOSITION

The Observer: Labour pledges 80 new rape courts to tackle backlog crisis

Some of us had received a request from a journalist at Channel 4 about their *Britain Decides* special programme on the night of the general election. Although we would all obviously be otherwise engaged at our respective counts, they were looking for people who might want to be part of the audience on the night and asked if we could recommend any Reform voices who might be interested in attending.

The invitation had come from an assistant producer who signed off as (name changed) Lara Brown (She/Her), which elicited the response from one of my colleagues that, "I wouldn't collaborate on a show with anyone who feels it necessary to publish their pronouns." Like him (Mr), I fail to understand what seems to me to be the ridiculous fixation whereby people feel the need to add a pronoun to their names when signing correspondence, to signify either their sex or sexuality. If a person is called Charles, I reckon there's a pretty good bet they are male (or at least identify as one...), and equally, if they are called Charlotte (or Lara...), there's a strong chance they are female.

Whether they are now the same sex as they were so-called 'assigned' at birth seems to me to be a total irrelevance, as indeed is their sexuality-which is simply providing 'too much information' that I have no need or desire to know, especially when it's presented to me at breakfast time while I'm checking incoming messages. If the sender is a 'Hemale' or a 'Shemale' is of no relevance to me and of even less interest. The notion that anyone can identify as an inanimate object like a car or a table is even more absurd and far-fetched, as is the idea that I could present myself as an animal or identify as a dog-and in that respect, it seems to me (no pun intended) that the world has gone barking mad.

This ludicrous idea was later perpetuated by the suggestion from the newly appointed Labour Health Minister,

Ashley Dalton, that people should be allowed to self-identify as a llama if they chose to do so. This begged the question in my mind as to whether those deluded in this way would also expect to eat grass and sleep on straw although the notion could be a reassuring one for our farmers if it led them to believe that any other similarly afflicted labour politicians might have a greater degree of empathy for the plight of their industry.

I sense that the obsession with diversity is now losing momentum, and that, in a partial return to normality, the questionable practice of adding preferred pronouns is now thankfully quietly dropping off email signatures. Some organisations, including the 'woke and broke' universities-already guilty of failing to offer value for money-are apparently and mercifully dispensing with their 'Diversity and Inclusion' personnel, which would seem to be a better use of limited resources currently being misspent on this sort of nonsense.

We are already subjected to watching fictitious young black couples on TV with rainbow-coloured offspring advertising something (which gets completely lost in the distraction) and serves only to make most of us confused and alienated, because blended families like that simply don't exist in the real world.

It came as no great surprise that Reform's very refreshing promise to dispense with, and for society to no longer be held hostage to, the "woke" ideology that had reached a crescendo in recent years was enthusiastically welcomed by almost all with whom I met and engaged with.

***

Sean reported that my bio was now in the process of being approved and that it should soon be uploaded onto the requisite page on the Reform website with the initial candidate information on me. He also assured me that, once the NDA and GDPR hoops were jumped through, IT would be able to provide me with a domain email address and access to the Nation Builder database.

However, I had already asked again if they could arrange the course in the next couple of days, but they failed to come up with extra dates, and I had already been told by the East Midlands Regional Manager, Helen O'Hare, that the next one was not until next Sunday-which would leave me very little time to campaign.

***

The membership of Reform UK had now increased to over 40,000. In the meantime, a poll conducted for *The Independent*, surveying 2,000 adults, had revealed that Nigel was the top choice to take over as Conservative leader if (or rather *when*...) Labour won the GE.

It was reported that almost one in five voters (19%) thought he should take over, and more surprisingly, that 22% of 2019 Conservative voters supported the idea.

The Tory Party needed Reform as much as the rest of the country.

Monday 10th June

Front Pages:

The Times: Tories must embrace Farage, says Braverman

The Daily Telegraph: Sunak pledges to put 8,000 more bobbies on the beat

i: Labour yet to convince voters on key policy areas, poll shows

The Guardian: Macron calls snap election after surge of far right

Financial Times: Labour throws out proposal to bring back lifetime cap on tax-free pensions

I was being asked with increasing frequency by people who now had my personal email address, including members of the press, about the lack of my biography on the party website, which was incredibly frustrating. With no details available for anyone to view, I was the invisible man, but I finally received a cheery message from Dave Holland telling me that he would upload it as soon as it had been approved. I could hardly contain my composure but was wise not to hold my breath for it to happen...

In the course of my business of raising debt and equity funding for SMEs, a field that I was keen to support as they represent the vast majority of businesses in the UK, I had what was scheduled to be a half-hour Zoom call with one of the investment banks with whom I was in the process of arranging a multi-million-pound debt facility for a corporate client who were negotiating to buy a large Northamptonshire-based engineering company. In fact, it turned into a one-and-a-half-hour call, and most of the extended conversation was taken up with a political debate, with me being quizzed by my contacts there on the merits of the party and how we proposed to "Reform" the country and its governance.

Once again, to my surprise, I received a very favourable reception from my two contacts, both of whom hold senior positions in the City and were unashamedly Lib Dem voters. Each of them told me later that, after our dialogue-which had given them so much to think about-they would be voting for their local Reform MP. Gratifying for me, but of course it wouldn't help my own vote, although I was aware that it was beholden on me and other candidates to act in an ambassadorial capacity for the good of the party.

The more conversations I had with a variety of people from all sorts of different backgrounds, the more I became aware of the diversity of opinions and issues that mattered to people when it came to voting for a new government. And of course, it helped me to refine my personal sales pitch and presentation once I was in a position to start engaging with voters on a formal basis.

***

Reform UK held a press conference in which Party Chairman Richard Tice quoted *Capital Economics*, a consultancy who estimated that the government could save up to £40 billion a year if the BoE scrapped the payment of all interest on bank reserves.

Under its quantitative easing economic stimulus, the central bank had bought £875 billion of government bonds that pay a fixed interest rate, which it paid for with cash on which it pays interest at its main interest rate, now at a 16-year high. He said the plan would speed up the economy and end the "gross negligence" of the BoE paying tens of billions of pounds a year to banks under its QE scheme, funded by taxpayers. He stressed that, “This is real cash, your money, being used to enrich the City of London."

Reform UK were now sitting third in pre-election opinion polls and, compounding the woes of the Conservatives, reiterated that it wanted to lift the annual threshold at which people start to pay income tax from £12,570 to a minimum of £20,000.

Taxes were at the highest level for 70 years, and this would free up 7 million people from paying any income tax and get them back into work. Making work pay better than living off the bloated welfare system was central to my belief that this would not only be good for the economy but also for the morale and health of workers.

Ian Gribbin, who was the Reform UK candidate for the Bexhill and Battle constituency, apologised and "unreservedly" withdrew comments that he'd made in an old internet post suggesting that Britain should have taken Hitler up on his offer of neutrality instead of fighting the Nazis during the Second World War.

He said that he was "upset" about how they had been "taken out of context" and further apologised for the distress they had caused, pointing out that his mother was the daughter of Russian Jewish people who'd fled persecution.

Despite this, there was no doubt that the comments were inappropriate and ill-advised, and something which the party could ill afford.

When asked about the comments at a press conference later, Tice said that if people did “inappropriate things” or said “daft things”, the party would “look at it” and “investigate", whilst Farage made the justifiable point that "every party" would face issues with vetting candidates due to the unexpected election timing, which had cut short the checks that all parties should carry out.

Tuesday 11th June

Front Pages:

Daily Mirror: Keir Starmer: MY PLEDGE ON KIDS’ HEALTH

The Daily Telegraph: Sunak offers tax break to landlords

The Times: Tories offer lower taxes and help for homebuyers

The Guardian: Tory right plans to give Sunak set of demands if manifesto falls flat

Daily Express: PM vows to slash welfare bill with ANOTHER tax reduction

i: Sunak hopes on NI cut to rescue stricken Tory campaign

Financial Times: Labour’s reluctance to rule out capital gains tax rise stokes investment fears

The media bias against Reform was vociferous in its condemnation of Ian Gribbin. Inevitably, the newspapers had a field day and linked the remarks to their repetitive narrative that Reform UK were racist, whilst conveniently ignoring the fact that Nigel Farage's wife is German.

Until his comments were made public yesterday, I had no idea that he was standing as a candidate, although I did recognise his name from somewhere. After trawling through my emails from the dim and distant past, in a quirk of fate, I confirmed that I had indeed come into contact with him twenty years previously, as he worked in Tokyo as a trader for Credit Suisse and, as Managing Director, I would have been indirectly involved in his recruitment.

Although deputy leader Ben Habib had told *Times Radio* today that the party's senior management had decided that the comments were "not worthy of any future action", I had no wish to be associated in any way with him or his remarks, even if they were out of date and out of context and so . I was relieved that an over-enthusiastic cub reporter didn't think to add two and two together to make five and imply that I was guilty by association. Other than as distant former colleagues (albeit in a vast organisation), there was no connection between us, but it was a stark reminder of both the powers and risks of social media.

There was a lot of dialogue between the other candidates on the Northants WhatsApp group as to whether or not they'd been invited to any hustings, but of course, as I was yet to have access to my Reform email address, I was embarrassed that I had no way of knowing whether or not I had been asked to appear at any kind of events.

What was even more exasperating was that although my name had now finally been added to the party website for Kettering, there were still no other details by way of profile or biography. Having written it myself and delivered it to the requisite factotum, I discovered it all needed to be cleared by the area manager, Helen O'Hare. In order to try and accelerate the process, I played an incredibly tedious game of cat and mouse over email and telephone, with each of them blaming the other for the lack of progress.

When I did eventually speak to Helen that evening, I discovered that she was not only regional manager for the East Midlands area but, like so many others that I had contact with in the party, she was also busy looking after her own affairs, doubling up as a PC.

It emerged that she obviously knew absolutely nothing about me and, whilst perfectly courteous, just assumed that I was throwing my hat into the ring as a 'Paper Candidate'.[22]

---

[22] *A paper candidate is someone who stands for a political party in an electoral constituency where their party enjoys a low level of support, lends it their name, and generally has no chance of winning, but enables the party to at least have representation on the ballot paper for supporters to vote for. They are also known as 'no-hope candidates'!*

However, I made it clear that I felt very strongly about the party, it's policies and all that it stood for and assured her that, whilst I still had my hands tied behind my back, I was taking the responsibility extremely seriously. It wasn't her fault that she didn't already know about me, but it was symptomatic of the lack of communication, organisation (and unprofessionalism?) that the future party chairman, Zia Yusuf, would later publicly acknowledge and seek to redress.

Nevertheless, I found her uninformed comments dismissive and demoralising and was even more underwhelmed when she made it very clear that, irrespective of my enthusiasm, I stood no hope of getting much traction. The priorities in the region were to win seats for the higher-profile Richard Tice (Boston and Skegness) and Ben Habib (Wellingborough), who, like NF, had served as an MEP.

She said that all and any of the limited resources that were available would be steered in their direction, which was fair enough, and that my time would be better spent supporting them - but that was not what I was doing this for. I may not have been an experienced politician (and nor was she...), but I was investing considerable time and energy in the party and didn't appreciate the lack of respect and being patronised like a nobody by someone considerably younger than me, especially as I was already meeting and talking to constituents and acting as a sounding board for the party.

She went on to stress that any votes won would be for Reform or for Farage and not for me or any of the other individual candidates (although her arrogance and sense of self-importance was such that I assume she naturally excluded herself and her own Sherwood Forest constituency in her calculations), all of whom had put in so much work selling the virtues of the party and their policies to make Britain great again. It was as though she was willing me to fail and, whilst she may have been correct to some extent, this was not good people management - and in my case, it was like a red rag to a bull. If nothing else, her comments strengthened my resolve and motivated me to prove her wrong in Kettering. And I did so.

As well as her extraordinarily discouraging stance, she made it very clear that she didn't feel it within her remit or interest to give me any guidance as to how to conduct or coordinate an election campaign. In retrospect, she was probably as much in the dark as I was, so from my perspective this wasn't even a courtesy call so much as a waste of time in my vain attempt to get someone, whose title implied that she was supposedly higher up the food chain, and who I naively assumed had sufficient influence, to pull strings and get me onto an earlier GDPR course and my details up on the website.

***

Reform UK were now only two points behind the Tories in the latest YouGov survey.

Farage was quoted in *The Daily Telegraph* as saying, “I won’t join the Tories... they’ll join us,” but meanwhile was out on the campaign trail in the open-top ‘Battle Bus’ and under physical attack for a second time, this one more serious than the previous incident in Clacton. He narrowly avoided being hit by wet cement and a cup, which were thrown at him while he was in Barnsley, South Yorkshire, by a 28-year-old man who was immediately arrested.

In thanking the local police, Farage described the attack as: "A wilful attempt to stop me taking part in this general election," and said that: “I will not be bullied or cowed by a violent left-wing mob who hates our country.”

Rishi unveiled the Conservative manifesto at the Silverstone race circuit in Northamptonshire, which is a place not only close to my home but also to my heart. It’s my local track and where, to borrow a phrase from the late, great world champion racing driver Niki Lauda, I have spent so much time “driving around in circles getting nowhere very fast” - something which could also be used as an apt description for what the Conservative Party had been doing for the last fourteen years.

It was an interesting choice of venue, justified by Sunak claiming that the setting showed the "power of the British economy", but despite my love of the former World War II airfield, I was not alone in being unable to make the connection.

He told the assembled audience that he was "not blind to the fact that voters were frustrated with the Tories, with him personally, and that the government hadn't got everything right", which was something of an understatement. Separately, he had told voters: "If you don't know what Labour will do, don't vote for them. If you're concerned about what Starmer isn't telling you, don't vote for them." The same message could, of course, also be applied to him and his own party. By this time, many of his MPs facing an uncertain future were already more concerned about who would be their next leader and whether or not they would hang on to their jobs.

Rachel Reeves was the third member of Labour's powerful and highly dangerous triumvirate, and she dismissed the Conservative manifesto as a "desperate wish list of unfunded promises". Yet within only a few months of her stewardship as Chancellor, it would be her responsibility - and opportunity - to screw things up, something she wholeheartedly embraced with both hands.as she completely lost control of public spending

If "Sterile Starmer" was dull as the proverbial ditchwater, then Reeves could be described as being shallow as a puddle. But like Rayner, she is a firebrand class warrior who also murders the English language with her strangulated vowel sounds.

Within weeks of becoming the (good for very little) Chancellor of the Exchequer, she would also start murdering our economy by proving herself hopelessly out of her depth and financially illiterate, with her creative accounting about the true size of the deficit. Not only was she guilty of making things up as she went along when it came to the economy, but opposition MPs would subsequently claim that she was a charlatan who had been "creative" and economical with the truth about her subsequently "updated" CV.[23]

When these allegations came to light, they cast even more doubt on whether she was suitably qualified to be Chancellor any more than she was to be an astronaut.

---

[23] *Rachel Reeves: A BBC investigation found that she had repeatedly overstated the length of time that she had worked at the Bank of England as an economist. She claimed it was for almost a decade, when in fact she had only been there for 5.5 years, one of which was spent attending a course at the LSE. More criticism about claims that she had previously worked, also as an economist, at HBOS led to her LinkedIn CV being edited to "Retail Banking" where she reportedly ran a small customer complaints team.*

Whatever the truth, "Rachel from Accounts", as she soon became known, and despite boastful claims about her formidable experience as an economist, drove the country at high speed towards a fiscal car crash and was condemned for her economic policies, contained within her first budget. These would go on to devastate British businesses and clearly prove that she had learnt nothing from her experience of working in the field of 'customer complaints' at HBOS.

The exaggerated entries on her CV were analogous to a porn star claiming to be a qualified gynecologist and which, in any other job would lead to instant dismissal. Once confirmed in the job, she took every opportunity to demonstrate appalling judgement and would become flawless at getting things wrong, as she showed that the biggest obstacle to economic growth was herself - with the consequent lack of credibility reflected in plummeting personal ratings.

NF was interviewed on the BBC's *Panorama* programme, for which the broadcaster received complaints about the bias displayed by their presenter Nick Robinson. They chose not to release any comment on it - until the day after the election.

Wednesday 12th June

Front pages:

Daily Express: TORY AMBITION TO DEPORT 100,000 ILLEGAL IMMIGRANTS

Daily Mail: RISHI: DON'T GIVE LABOUR A BLANK CHEQUE

The Times: PM: A vote for Reform puts Labour into No 10

The Daily Telegraph: Sunak promises £17bn in tax cuts

The Guardian: Tories' 'implausible' £17nb tax giveaway condemned

The Independent: Sunak's final gamble: I'll cut taxes by 17bn and migration by 50%

i: Labour promises £12 an hour to care workers

Financial Times: Sunak's £17bn tax cuts promise fails to satisfy Tory appetite for 'boldness'

Daily Mirror: SUNAK'S IDEA OF HARDSHIP RISHI I DIDN'T HAVE A DISH

Despite my entreaties to the area manager, who had resolved to try and accelerate the process of getting me onto the elusive GDPR course as soon as possible, and also to get my bio posted onto the party website, there was still no progress with either. I sent her a repetitious email chasing her up yet again.

Whether or not she ever got around to doing so, it was me who finally managed to get to him first and tracked down the self-important factotum in IT who was tasked with posting my bio. He was unnecessarily abrupt, to the point of being extremely rude. His excuse was that he had over 600 of these to do and so mine would have to wait in the queue whilst he (also 'moonlighting' as yet another PPC himself...) found time to upload it.

This was disingenuous because, and no pun intended, I had been so late to the party in every respect that, by the time mine had been approved, the majority of my colleagues' profiles had already been uploaded for weeks - many of them before the election had even been called. I felt it likely that my verbal spat with him resulted in him purposely delaying my entry onto the website even longer, as it was within his power to ensure that I fell even further down his list of priorities. He made it clear that he had "enough to do without speaking to people like you" which was both unnecessary and unhelpful!

This was yet another indication of the lack of support afforded to mere mortals like me who were desperately trying to do their best for party and country. In fairness, it was symptomatic of the pressures people were under and another manifestation of the shortage of manpower that the short notice of the election had caused, especially for

Reform. It was also another very clear indication that, even within the party, it was every man or woman for themselves. I was beginning to feel as though there was a conspiracy to ensure that I failed and, whilst recognizing that everyone else was busy too, I was increasingly disheartened to feel that I had such limited support.

The only piece of useful information that I received from the area manager had been a reference to a Police Security Briefing, which had been given to candidates the previous evening - but which I obviously had no knowledge of, as I was still a week away from being given access to my email or other communication.

The gist of the presentation, from Superintendent Scott Little, had been to raise our awareness of various safety measures that should be taken, and to request that, if we were attending any hustings, talks or Q&A events, we should inform the police of their location and timings in advance.

There has been an alarming rise in the intimidation of political candidates and campaigners over the years. Despite the memory of the appalling murders of MPs Jo Cox in 2016 and Sir David Amess in 2021, it had never occurred to me to be concerned about my personal safety. Until the subject was raised, I hadn't considered the prospect of being subjected to any threats or physical violence.

The targeting of MPs, candidates or their families is completely unacceptable and contradicts democratic rights because if it deters people from standing, then by definition it impacts democracy, giving voters less choice.

Mercifully, this country doesn't have the gun culture that exists in the US. However, the issue was brought into sharp focus when, within two weeks of our election, there was an assassination attempt on Republican presidential nominee and former President Donald Trump. The poor turnout of candidates across parties at hustings reflected their fears of recrimination and intimidation.

In my case, most of the abuse I would receive was not on the streets or face-to-face, but online. I was, of course, mindful that not everyone I met or spoke to would welcome me or my opinions. I took note of the two assaults on Nigel early in his campaign and, although I was prepared for some abuse, I was rarely heckled by more than a handful of people. I was surprised that I didn't have so much as a rotten egg or tomato thrown at me bearing in mind how much time I was to spend 'loitering with intent' outside supermarkets, talking to shoppers who were armed with all manner of recently bought goods that they could have used as 'ammunition' to hurl in my direction. Their restraint was a welcome surprise, and I was grateful for their good manners but it did not disguise the strongly held views of voters.

Others fared less well, including the Labour MP Jonathan Ashworth, who said that he had "never known of a campaign of such vitriol, bullying, and intimidation," and revealed to LBC radio that he had been forced to seek refuge in a vicarage after being chased down the street. He said that it was a horrible campaign and that he'd never known one of such aggression and violence.

I was new to all of this and had no preconceptions of what to expect. Whilst I fully expected more heckling or even verbal abuse than I got, I clearly escaped lightly and enjoyed engaging with (almost) everybody that I met in person - although less so with some of the cowards online, of which more later.

Ashworth also claimed that tactics were beyond normal or acceptable. In my case, the worst 'dirty tricks' that I encountered was witnessing volunteers removing the flyers for rival candidates that hadn't been properly, and often painfully, poked through letterboxes.

Thinking that my profile as a 'politician' had risen to such an extent that I was being recognised in the streets of Kettering, I was briefly quite flattered when a man from another party acknowledged me by saying, "You're Crispian Besley, aren't you?" My momentarily inflated ego was swiftly brought back down to earth when I realised that the most likely reason he knew that was from the awful photo he had seen on one of my leaflets, which he had presumably just 'liberated' and was now scrunched up in his pocket!

***

In his latest faux pas, Rishi told ITV - with a straight face - that he knew what it was like to struggle, as he had been deprived of lots of things when growing up as a child, including Sky TV!

If this was designed to win empathy or suggest that he'd come from an impoverished background, it completely backfired. There are tens of millions of households (mine included) that still don't have a Sky account. This precipitated more memes and cartoons ridiculing "No Dishi Rishi", confirming that he was out of touch with the people.

Conservative MP Dame Andrea Jenkyns[24] defended her choice of featuring a photo of herself with Nigel Farage at his 60th birthday in April on her personal election leaflet, rather than one of the PM, of whom she had been a vocal critic and had submitted a letter of no confidence in 2023.

She had been a staunch Brexiteer, calling for her party to unite with Reform to prevent a Labour "supermajority" and "the end of Britain as we know it".

---

[24] *Having lost her seat in the 2024 General Election Andrea Jenkyns defected to Reform UK on 28th November 2024 saying that the Conservative party was now "beyond salvage" but that Reform were "patriotic bravehearts" who would "deliver the fresh start this country so desperately needs".*

Thursday 13th June

Front pages:

The Times: Growth and prosperity our priority, says Starmer

Daily Express: RISHI: IF YOU CARE ABOUT TAX CUTS AND PROTECTING PENSIONS, ONLY I CAN DELIVER

The Daily Telegraph: Starmer paves the way for tax rises

Daily Mail: A TORY WIPEOUT RISKS ONE-PARTY SOCIALIST STATE

The Guardian: Sunak aide bet on election date before announcement

i: Labour set to announce big cuts to public services in UK

There were now only 21 days to go and if I'd had hair left, I would have been pulling it out by then, as there was still no sign of my bio or any details on the website. Messages from the appropriately named Dave Holland were all "double Dutch" to me as they implied an unwillingness and inability to help but more likely were just an indication that he was just too "busy" orchestrating his own campaign, so I asked Sean if he could reach out to anybody in IT who could find the necessary two minutes that it would surely take to do it.

In the meantime, my fumbling efforts to engage on social media had resulted in me setting up a Reform UK page for

Kettering on Facebook, which gave me something else to do. I don't consider myself superstitious, but it might have been better if I hadn't chosen the 13th of the month to do it but at least it wasn't Friday the 13th and I did find it a useful platform from which to relay party messages to people.

My first post was along the lines of naively asking people what they'd prefer: 'Starmergeddon' or a real alternative to save Britain by voting Reform? This slightly backfired on me, as it invited several tongue in cheek responses in favour of "Starmergeddon please!" These were accompanied by smiley-faced emoji's, which I could safely presume didn't come from Reform voters. Although they were more by way of humour, I suppose I had only myself to blame for inadvertently inviting that sort of response. To which my less-than-humorous reply was: "Be careful what you wish for. Labour have proved to be totally inept and ineffectual in opposition over the last 14 years; the Conservatives have broken Britain with their policies, Labour will break it. Reform is needed, etc. etc."

Sadly, not long after my Facebook page went live, a directive from Regional Office was circulated asking that candidates should stop sharing memes, as they were deemed to be neither professional nor helpful. It was understandable, but rather a shame, as I had enjoyed reading some of those that I received from others.

There was lots of talk between the Northants PCs that, with three weeks to go, the belief was that Reform now represented His Majesty's unofficial opposition in the campaign, which was a very exciting thought. Starmer had started to make oblique references to Clacton by suggesting that those who wanted "Pantomime Politics" should go and watch Reform in Clacton-surely a sign that he was suddenly taking notice of the threat from Farage, but presumably he couldn't bring himself to mention the 'F word'. This may have been by way of returning a 'compliment' as our leader had already described Starmer as "Blair without the Flair"[25] in reference to Tony Blair who was the last Labour PM to have been elected.

It was through the WhatsApp group that I discovered that I needed to get some customised leaflets printed and was able to use the design and content of one of my new colleagues (Antony), who was very helpful and directed me to the same printing company that he had used. It was a surprise to me that there didn't seem to be a uniform design or template handed down from Party HQ, and apparently no restrictions or process to check what I actually put on it,

---

[25] *Sir Tony Blair was Leader of the Labour Party from 1994 and Prime Minister from 1997 to 2007. He is the second longest serving PM in post-war British history after Margaret Thatcher Also the longest serving Labour PM and the one to take the party to three consecutive general election victories.*

which all seemed remarkably hit-and-miss. However, I was very happy not to present the party "machine" with another unwelcome opportunity to exercise its interminable checking process, as the prospect of anything else being delayed didn't bear thinking about.

There was no directive as to which words or policy statements to include or highlight, and not even a stipulation as to what colour they should be, although I thought it appropriate to stick to the garish turquoise blue of the second-hand rosettes that Sean had dusted down and passed on to me. The only legal requirement appeared to be to include the "imprint" on it, defined as the name and address of the printers together with that of the party and my agent. The design also included one of the photographs of me looking hung-over, the party logo, and a few words including some major Reform UK themes of controlling immigration, ending the lunacy of net zero, fixing waiting lists and raising the personal taxation threshold.

The next revelation was that I was expected to pay for these out of my own pocket, together with any other expenses incurred! It hadn't occurred to me that I was expected to fund my own personal campaign to the benefit of the party. Up until now, it had been underwritten by a handful of generous benefactors, of which Richard Tice was one of the largest single donors, as well as subscriptions and donations from its rapidly expanding membership. No one had warned me that their coffers were so low that I presumed (but never confirmed) every other candidate was expected to do so too.

Individual expenditure was limited by law to no more than £20,000 per candidate, but with the little money that my ex-wife had left me with, there was no chance of me being able to afford that amount, so that was never going to be an issue. Neither did I have any idea as to how many of these leaflets to have printed, but I knew I couldn't afford one for every household, let alone every person on the electoral roll in my patch. Even if I had been able to, in the limited time now available it would have been impossible to deliver them all. Taking the lead from my WhatsApp 'team-mates', I decided on 20,000 and went through what should have been a simple ordering process, but which, because of the inefficiencies of the feckless printers I'd been recommended, turned into a painfully laborious and frustrating one. Eventually, I finally received confirmation of my order, followed by several more communications that they were 'working' on it, followed by another saying that it was ready to be dispatched the next day which was a relief, although this turned out to be short lived.

***

On LBC Radio this morning, Nigel Farage told Nick Ferrari that he would be willing to lead a merged Conservative-Reform political party in the guise of the official opposition to the forthcoming Labour government. It was an intriguing idea, and I entertained myself thinking up hypothetical names for the newly merged entity. I decided that, while "Conform" might be preferable to "Refory" and "Recon" would have unfortunate connotations, nothing could beat the name of our party, Reform, which so accurately described what our country needs. In any case, our supporters don't want to see a rehash of the Conservatives; they are hungry for change and demand Reform, with a capital R!

In another blow to the Tories' election campaign, a YouGov poll of public opinion showed that, in a "crossover" moment between the two, Reform (19%) had now overtaken the Conservatives (18%) for the first time.

In an identical line-up to the first seven-way debate on BBC One the previous week, ITV hosted a second one. Another blow to the Tories' election campaign had been the YouGov poll, which showed that in a "crossover" moment between the two, Reform (19%) had now overtaken the Conservatives (18%) for the first time. This prompted Nigel to introduce himself: "I am Nigel Farage, leader of Reform UK. Just before we came on air, we overtook the

Conservatives in the national opinion polls. We are now the opposition to Labour!" He also said that he'd come out of retirement with "passion in his heart," pointing out that Starmer would win the election but reiterated his previous point by laying down the gauntlet and posing the question: who would be the leader of the opposition? He also blamed an "exploding population" for the increase in pressure on the NHS, saying that it "has two fundamental problems": firstly, that caseloads were up by 43%, and secondly, that all of our public services had been impacted by the explosion in population by six million since the Conservatives came to power.

Penny Mordaunt, soon to be the ex-leader of the House of Commons, correctly accused Labour of wanting to raise taxes, while at the same time saying that they had no economic plans. "You've had 14 years to come up with some ideas," she said, to which Angela Rayner tripped her up by replying, "You've had 14 years in government..." This brought to mind the comments made by the late Sir Keith Joseph[26] in 1976, during a Labour government, when he said that fourteen years in power had left Britain "over-governed, over-spent, over-taxed, and over-borrowed."

---

[26] *Sir Keith Joseph was a member of the Conservative Party and served as a minister under four prime ministers including Margaret Thatcher. He was a key architect of what became known as Thatcherism.*

Whilst not endorsing any of Mr Gribbin's comments, Nigel Farage tried to brush them off with an unconvincing suggestion that he'd probably only been making "ordinary folk down the pub speak," and blamed the PM's decision to call a snap election for not giving parties sufficient time to properly vet candidates. He declined to say whether he still backed rogue candidates, saying "I can disown them, I might well do that," but pointed out that he wasn't able to deselect Gribbin because he was already on the ballot paper, and the legal deadline had passed for withdrawing prospective MPs.

An apology came from Conservative candidate Craig Williams, who was the PM's PPS, admitting that he'd made a "huge error of judgement" over betting on the date of the next general election. It was alleged that he had placed a £100 bet on a July election three days before Rishi Sunak announced the 4 July poll. Sunak's decision to call the poll was a surprise to most, including his own MPs, who were expecting an autumn date but obviously not to him. This further served to discredit the Tory campaign.

Friday 14th June

Front pages:

The Daily Telegraph: Reform overtakes Tories for first time

Independent: Starmer taunts Tories: Labour is the party of wealth creation now

Daily Express: DON'T FALL FOR LABOUR'S HIDDEN £8.5BN 'TAX TRAP'

Daily Mail: WHAT IS LABOUR NOT TELLING US ABOUT TAX HIKES?

The Times: 'Conspiracy of silence' on cuts and higher taxes

The Guardian: I'll fix Britain, vows Starmer amid doubts over how he will pay for it

Daily Mirror: STARMER'S MANIFESTO. WE'LL GIVE NATION HOPE

i: Labour overtakes Tories on defence - but gets reality check on growing UK economy

Financial Times: Starmer unveils £6.8bn tax hit in bid to revive growth and end Tory 'chaos'

Joy of joys, and admittedly better late than never, my biography had finally been approved. Despite my spat with the PC i/c of IT, it had now been uploaded onto the Reform UK website, which was a great relief. However, I couldn't understand why it had taken so long, as it was hardly a 'magnum opus' or the length of Tolstoy's *War and Peace*, and it contained reference to several of the party's policies.

Now, the whole world had access to a picture of me (looking disfigured!) and an email address through which to contact me, but which I still hadn't gained access to myself, so I couldn't reply to anyone! I shuddered to think of how many accumulated messages would be waiting for me if I were ever to be given access.

I also received acknowledgement from the self important but undermanned and inefficient NDA team (which probably only consisted of one man and his dog) that they had finally processed the elusive document and filed it successfully. Over the course of my career in banking and business, I had signed dozens of these every year but had lost count of the number of times I had been asked to (re)send in my signed forms, which had either gone into spam or got lost in the ether somewhere. The receipt of this was another prerequisite for access to party data or receiving the occasional update/daily file of reactions and recommended responses to the media landscape, which only added to my frustration. But, in fairness, I still didn't fully comprehend the lack of resources the party was operating under. As a result, I also felt that the eleven-day delay in rebooking me for the GDPR session was unacceptable, although I hoped that at least this would give me immediate access to my Reform email address and enable me to ramp up my activities for the last two weeks of the campaign.

Contradicting their assurances from the previous day, after the close of business, the lackadaisical printers, without any concern, explanation, or apology, sent me a notification of changes to my delivery. This was despite having charged me a premium for their so-called 'express' service. This delayed my plans for leaflet distribution by yet another day, and it seemed that inefficiencies and circumstances were again conspiring against me. I was going to have even less time to run a meaningful campaign.

This evening, another (again inexplicably unrecorded) Zoom call was missed by me and presumably by the majority of other hardworking Reform PCs, who would have been pounding the streets of their respective constituencies. It would have been helpful to have heard the presentations on best practices in the use of social media and the guidance on keeping on-message with the party's policy positions.

***

The halfway point in the six-week election campaign had now been reached. Polling cards were arriving at people's doors, and the first postal votes could be cast. Yet, I still hadn't been able to start campaigning. Including me (!), there were more than 4,500 candidates standing, and no seat had fewer than five to choose from. The biggest change from 2019 was the number of 609 that Reform UK was fielding. The election dynamic had changed, and our party didn't even need to win seats to damage the Conservatives.

At a press conference in Westminster, Nigel Farage declared himself the real "leader of the opposition" and optimistically predicted his party would gain more than 6 million votes at the election. He believed that they'd gain more votes than the Tories after polling ahead of them for the first time. He confirmed the momentum behind the party and claimed we were significantly ahead of them in the 'red wall' seats. The Tory reaction to the YouGov poll showing that they'd been overtaken by Reform, who were now in second place-one point ahead with 19%-was muted.

He also took the opportunity to criticise the Ofcom rules, in which the allocation of broadcast election coverage is based on performance during the last two elections, in which Reform did not stand. He claimed that this was designed to maintain the status quo and showed that our political system was set up to prevent "new boys and girls from coming in and to keep everything the same."

He also demanded that the BBC allow him to take part in a leaders' debate next week and challenged Starmer to a head-to-head debate on immigration so that he could ask the question that Rayner hadn't been able to answer in the most recent TV debate the previous evening: Why wasn't immigration one of his "six steps" of government?

Saturday 15th June

Front pages:

i Weekend: Tories face growing peril from Farage

The Guardian: Tory leadership hopefuls jostle to replace Sunak

The Independent: Rattled Sunak tries to calm Tory nerves over march of Farage

A fantastic milestone was reached by the party, with our membership surpassing 50,000, which was a testament to the momentum we were building. However, to add to my frustration, I learned that our database suggested that 389 of them were registered in the Kettering constituency. But of course, I still didn't have access to most of them. Thankfully, due to Sean's earlier quest to get signatories for my candidacy, several had already gained access to my personal email address, and so I was already engaged in dialogue with some of them-many of whom would become really helpful allies and had kindly volunteered to help distribute my leaflets for me. If and when they ever arrived.

My frustrations continued when, lacking any sense of urgency, the ultra-relaxed anonymous printing company informed me of changes to my delivery date, moving it from Monday 17th to Tuesday 18th June. Every day was now critical, and I could ill afford to lose another day. So, I spent much of the weekend exchanging after-hours messages, calling various numbers, and contacting their unresponsive and inaccurately described 24/7 hotline, all to no avail.

***

In an interview with *The Times*, the Foreign Secretary, Lord Cameron, claimed that Nigel Farage was trying to destroy the Conservatives and criticised his "inflammatory language" on migration. He said: "I think with these populists, what you get is inflammatory language and hopeless policy," and also warned that a vote for Reform or any other party would make "Britain less safe." What he omitted to say on immigration was that his own party was responsible for allowing far too many people to use our country as an all-expenses-paid hotel. Some school children I spoke to were quick to understand that, in their words, our country is "full up," and that an influx of 700,000 immigrants each year was not sustainable-especially when only 20% of them were contributing to the economy through work and paying taxes.[27] The equation is not exactly rocket science, and if school kids can work it out, then why are so many politicians in denial about facing the facts and addressing the problems that previous governments have created, remaining too scared to address them?

---

[27] *The most recent figures released by the ONS suggested a net (!) immigration figure of 1.2million people as of the end of June 2024 which for a country with an existing population of about 68.5 million is economically unsustainable.*

In the first MRP analysis since Farage announced that he'd be standing for election after all, Reform UK were leading in seven seats and were currently placed second, within 10 points of the leading candidate in six more.

Sunday 16th June

Front pages:

The Sunday Times: PM: Faith and duty guide me through my election trials

It was Father's Day, and the eldest of my two sons had very kindly travelled up from London by train to take the "old man" out for a lovely lunch at a local pub. He had recently got engaged, and although he had confided in me several weeks before that he had popped the question to his fiancée, we had lots to catch up on-discussing the excitement of his wedding plans, his new job offer, and the most recent Formula One Grand Prix. Inevitably, the conversation also included politics. Although a contrarian in some respects, he certainly would not have voted Reform solely because of my involvement in the party, but he definitely agreed with enough of our policies to want to see change from the mess that the Tory government had got the country into. He was very clear about the ramifications for his generation (being on the cusp of being a millennial and

Gen Z), and I hoped that our candidate, where he voted in London, would be able to rely on his vote too.

Whilst he remained extremely proud that I was standing up for the principles I believed in and had initially suggested that it would be a great "addition to my CV" (even though I was far too old to be concerned about my employment history), the conversation that followed was in fact more about the potential ramifications that my (likely) brief involvement in politics would have on his own CV! He had been spooked by some of the negative and biased media coverage on Reform and was acutely aware of the power and destructive effects of social media if one got on the wrong side of it, as Gribbin and others had done.

Fortunately, I wasn't a subscriber to X (constantly and irritatingly referred to as "formerly known as Twitter"), nor was I 'on' Instagram, which I still believed was used primarily by people who wanted to show off by posting either photos of food they were just about to eat or boasting about where they were on holiday in a digital postcard sort of way. It was true that I was analogue when it came to tech generally and social media in particular, and my Luddite and age-related lack of appreciation for the power of social media would undoubtedly count against me securing even more votes than I actually did in my forthcoming campaign.

However, like a lot of middle-aged people, I did use both Facebook and WhatsApp, and he was understandably concerned that some of the puerile jokes I'd received in the past from people in motor racing groups that I might either have liked, forwarded, read, or commented on could be used against me in some way by the wider media. His worry, if this was to happen, was more about the impact on his own CV and that an association with me might work against him, his brother, and their cousins with future job applications due to erroneous and unjustifiable connotations with racist attitudes in the party and the possibility that in the screening process they might make unfair and wrong assumptions.

He'd read history at university and, although he didn't quite see me as a contemporary Oswald Mosley[28] he was very clear that I should "clean up" my Facebook page by deleting anything from the last 10 years that might be deemed remotely offensive or controversial. I was confident there were no skeletons in the cupboard but, appalled at the prospect of compromising my sons any more than their grasping mother had already done financially. It's fair to say that social media was, and still is, a largely unexplored continent for me. But I respected his views, which focused my mind, and I took him at his word to dutifully expunge them as he'd asked, whilst mindful that, because of the age

---

[28] *Sir Oswald Mosley was a British aristocrat and the youngest elected Conservative MP before he crossed the floor in 1922, joining the Labour Party. He rose to fame during the 1920s and '30s when he turned to fascism. He founded the British Union of Fascists (BUF) in 1932 and led it until its forced disbandment in 1940 when it was made illegal and he was imprisoned.*

gap between us, we were likely to have differing opinions as to what could be defined as funny let alone contentious.

I stayed up until the early hours giggling at some of the innocent jokes, memes, and posts that I had unwittingly liked or forwarded several years previously and laboriously set about deleting them just in case any of them might have been deemed to be discriminatory in any way. I found I had also forwarded a few harmless and possibly non-PC jokes to friends about ex-wives, but most of them were harmless enough and were about cars and motor racing. If they were rude about anything at all, it was only me expressing my strong opinions about the shortcomings of electric cars. Politically incorrect some of them may have been, but it was a reminder of the easily offended "snowflake" generation and the nanny state we now live in, where there might be a handful of people who are unable to deal with opposing opinions and might not share my rather puerile sense of humour.

Separately, my younger son also dropped in on the way back to London from a party he'd been to in North Yorkshire, and I was heartened to learn from him that almost everyone in his cohort and 25-year-old age group that he'd been with saw the common sense in what Reform were advocating. There were no guarantees as to how they would actually cast their votes come the 4th July, but ahead of my active campaigning, it was encouraging to know that the party and its policies were striking some resonance with younger voters too.

Unfortunately, I had to cut his visit short because that evening as I also finally attended the long-awaited GDPR session on Zoom, which, although likely to be extremely dull, I could hardly contain my excitement about much longer, as this should have been my passport to getting my campaign started. It was attended by about 40 other late-coming parliamentary candidates, the interaction with whom surprised and horrified me in equal measures. Some had defected from previously held roles in the Tory party, others were notable for displaying even more severe Luddite tendencies than I did when it came to the technological aspects of getting logged into it, which delayed the start of the briefing session for everyone else who had been patiently waiting for as long as twenty minutes for it to start. A small number of those who asked the host a series of extraordinarily inane and repetitive questions gave an insight into what the party had been up against when it came to filling as many constituency nominations as quickly as possible, demonstrating that in some cases, they had little choice other than to opt for quantity over quality. It was an interesting snapshot, although I was really more concerned that it just further delayed the already painfully tedious proceedings, which was not ideal on a Sunday night.

The main purpose of the call was to instruct us on the dos and don'ts of how to respond to and interact with communications from constituents. It also focused on how to access and get us up to speed with the rather clunky and not always reliable internal 'Nationbuilder' database of paid-up members and supporters in our respective constituencies. In most cases, these represented only a couple of hundred names, and although it was reassuring and helpful to have access to them, they were easy pickings who could surely be relied on to put their crosses in the right place on ballot day, and on that basis, I felt my efforts would be better directed elsewhere. I later discovered that several of my peers found the system as difficult and user-unfriendly as I did, and like me, never properly mastered its intricacies, so they were never able to fully exploit its dubious benefits anyway.

The GDPR training itself was a necessity, which was well delivered and quite straightforward, but like many others, I would have welcomed some basic guidance on campaigning protocol and what one should be prepared for, but there was none given. I'd been assured that having completed this course, I would immediately be given access to my email account, which was filling up on a daily basis. Wrong! Again, the IT resource was such that this was delayed by several more days.

I read with envy of Nigel's day of campaigning on the "Battle Bus" whilst my more humble steed stayed dormant for the moment but was ready to spring into action if and when the wretched leaflets ever arrived.

Sean passed on a warning that Tommy Robinson[29] had endorsed both Nigel and Reform UK on social media, and because of his association with the BNP, we were forbidden to like, follow, retweet, or engage with him in any way for fear of being drawn into a trap by our 'enemies' or anyone who might use it as ammunition against us or the party. I still wasn't entirely sure what 'retweeting' meant or entailed.

***

Rishi Sunak opened up to *The Sunday Times* about the strength his Hindu faith had given him to carry on during his gaffe-filled election campaign and wrote that, with his party languishing in the polls, he could do with some divine intervention. Having met Pope Francis at the G7 summit in Italy before the weekend, he'd joked that they hadn't had time for a "spiritual conversation."

The Mail on Sunday reported that, whilst Boris Johnson was busy completing his memoirs and preparing to celebrate his 60th birthday, he had decided that an early return to Parliament in a by-election was unwise. However, he gave

---

[29] *Tommy Robinson was a member of the BNP, a British fascist political party and is an anti-Islam campaigner and one of the UK's most prominent far-right activists.*

his backing and endorsement to all candidates who asked for it and was understood to be working with Tory Party headquarters.

Another casualty for Reform was the forced resignation of their PC in North West Essex after it emerged that he allegedly urged people to vote for the BNP. Grant St Clair-Armstrong had used a blog to post jokes involving racial slurs and made a joke about "female hormones," according to *The Times*. However, he told the BBC, "I have never supported the BNP. I think they are a disgusting organisation," and that he "bitterly" regretted the comments he'd made over fifteen years ago.

NF said that he did not find the comments acceptable but stressed he "was never a member of the BNP." This brought the subject of vetting back into the spotlight, and once again, he reiterated that the party had put a process in place for vetting candidates but blamed the calling of a snap election for cutting this short.

With former PM John Major in Hong Kong 2004

Rishi in the rain outside number 10 on the 22nd May 2024

Furious Farage Nigel after being "milkshaked" on the campaign trail.

Just one of 20,000 leaflets my team of helpers and I had to distribute.

Limited support from the party. I wasn't even sent a souvenir copy!

Nigel demonstrating to Parliamentary Candidates how to put their head above the parapet

Britain needs Reform

Rishi Sunak helped to sink the Conservative party

What we had to "look forward to" after the 2024 General Election

Richard Tice MP and deputy leader of Reform UK

General election 2024: Kettering[7]

Party	Candidate	Votes	%	± %
Alliance for Democracy and Freedom	Jehad Soliman Aburamadan			
Reform UK	Crispian George Besley			
Green	Emily Fedorowycz			
Independent	Jim Hakewill			
Conservative	Philip Hollobone			
SDP	Matthew Murphy			
Liberal Democrats	Sarah Ryan			
Labour	Rosie Wrighting			

The "Runners and Riders" for Kettering

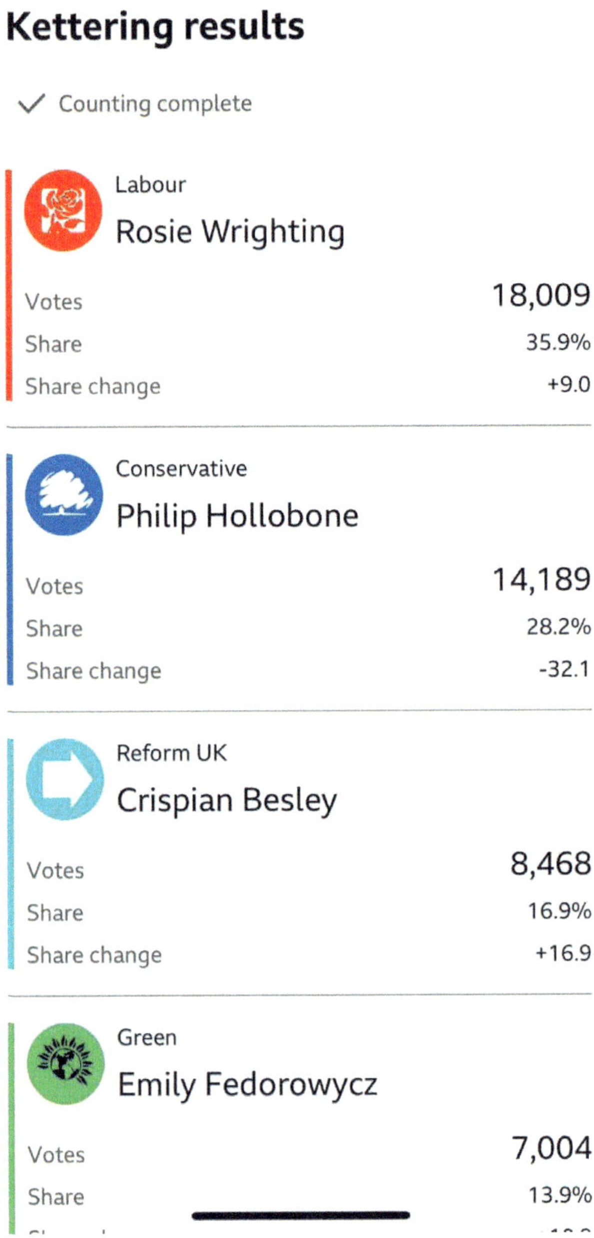

Kettering results

✓ Counting complete

Labour
Rosie Wrighting

Votes	18,009
Share	35.9%
Share change	+9.0

Conservative
Philip Hollobone

Votes	14,189
Share	28.2%
Share change	-32.1

Reform UK
Crispian Besley

Votes	8,468
Share	16.9%
Share change	+16.9

Green
Emily Fedorowycz

Votes	7,004
Share	13.9%

The final count

I never got to ride on the well travelled 'Battle Bus'

Election night with my agent, Sean Lever

Monday 17th June

Front pages:

The Independent: Mordaunt urges party to rally but admits Tories are underdogs

Daily Mirror: JUST THE JOB. Labour's plan for 650,000 new roles is unveiled

The Times: Go for the jugular, Sunak urged

Daily Express: PM: LABOUR WILL RUN RIOT WITH YOUR MONEY

The Daily Telegraph: Labour net zero plans £4.5bn tax black hole

Daily Mail: HAS LABOUR LET THE CAT OUT OF THE BAG ON TAX?

The Guardian: New calls on Starmer to discard Tories' two-child benefits limit

i: Labour accused of watering down housing reform pledges

Financial Times: Reeves pledges to tear down EU trade barriers in reset for relations

Despite paying them a premium for 'express' delivery of my leaflets, one of the first emails I received this morning was from the hapless but unjustifiably very merry printing company who seemed to find joy in their every error, happily proclaiming, "GREAT NEWS!" My delivery was going to be delivered by 8:00 pm tomorrow. It may have been "great news" for them, but it wasn't for me, as it would cost me yet another day's delay, which I could not afford with the limited time I had left to campaign. Having been promised them today, I had to reschedule all my meetings with my willing band of kindly volunteers-who had offered to deliver them on my behalf-to the next day. These leaflets were supposed to have been a critical part of my election campaign, so the delay had added yet another hurdle. The offer of a partial refund was of no consolation and didn't help me in the slightest. I now had only two weeks left to gather any form of support for myself and the party, so I was really feeling that the odds were stacked against me and that I was up against the wall.

I had spent my Sunday evening attending the on line GDPR meeting, from which I learned very little, other than the fact that there were quite a few other candidates who were even more incompetent than I was when it came to mastering technology. However, there was still no sign of my Kettering Reform email address being released to me or access to the much-vaunted party database. This was immensely frustrating, and I still had one hand tied behind my back as far as campaigning was concerned.

As a result, I had time for a quick pub lunch with a friend who lived in another constituency, but by the end of it, he had pledged his support for the party, so at least that was time well spent. I then met the South Northamptonshire candidate, Paul Hogan, for coffee in the sunshine outside another local pub. Although we had conversed, it was the first time that we had actually met. We got on very well and discussed our respective frustrations and campaigns, even though mine hadn't formally started at that point. As I was still restricted in terms of what I was allowed to do and in the absence of any of my own leaflets, I had time on my hands and was happy to offer to help one of my Northamptonshire candidate teammates by taking responsibility for distributing 300 of them for him in my own village. He was much more mellow in person than he'd been when we'd initially spoken on the phone, and his parting shot, which resonated with me over the coming weeks, was that had he realised how hard work it was, he would never have applied to be a candidate in the first place, which was something I rapidly came to understand and empathise with. Very graciously, he even told me that after the election, he'd be happy to step aside and let me take over the candidacy in his constituency, recognising that his age and levels of energy were likely to conspire against him.

My next meeting was at the business centre at the Silverstone racing circuit with my lawyer, who was someone who'd also been at school with me many years ago. After spirited debate with him about the state the country was in, I was unable to convince him of the logic of voting for Reform. Whilst he wholeheartedly agreed that the situation was untenable, he didn't warm to Nigel Farage and was resolutely sticking with the Lib Dems, even though he readily admitted that until recently, the party had maintained such a low profile that most of their supporters struggled to name their party leader, let alone his deputy. Over the course of his campaign the likeable but ineffectual Ed Davey did succeed in raising his own profile by getting his name and multiple photographs of himself in the media, less for what he said about his party's indeterminate policies and more by performing multiple stunts and generally making a fool of himself on constituency visits. This single-handedly reinforced the views of many that the House of Commons was indeed just a circus full of clowns.

The imaginative antics devised for the MP for Surbiton took place all over the country and included falling off a paddleboard several times in Lake Windermere in an attempt to highlight the sewage crisis, as well as taking part in yoga sessions and Zumba classes, water sliding and aerobics at Chessington, bungee jumping at Eastbourne

Borough FC, participating in multiple fun fair rides at various amusement parks and several activity centres. Amongst many other activities, he was also seen playing Frisbee in Fair Oak, 'racing' wheelbarrows in Yeovil, making sandcastles on a beach in Paignton, and baking cakes at a school in Harpenden. But no one really understood what message his cringing behaviour was trying to get across to voters. His disposition and avuncular manner would be very well suited to manning the tea and cakes stand at a sleepy village fete but if his advisors thought he was in some way emulating the macho action-man image of the egocentric Russian leader Vladimir Putin, they would have surely been disappointed. His activities might perhaps have been a good way of advertising tourism and leisure activities, but it was a strange way of attempting to build 'brand recognition' for a serious political entity. That said, his efforts to get himself noticed did at least serve to remind everyone that a party existed for those hesitant voters in a political no-man's land, who suffered from the inability to make a sensible decision. At least they were able to fulfil their moral obligation and responsibility to cast a vote, even if they didn't understand what they were actually voting for; Lib Dem policies were as clear as the mud in which the party leader had spent so much time clowning around in.

***

In the meantime, Nigel Farage was busy launching the Reform manifesto, together with Richard Tice, at a launch in the Welsh valleys. This prompted several 'humorous' messages from various friends, who asked me, with tongue firmly in cheek, if I'd be accompanying him on the journey to Wales. My riposte was that, similar to the fate of many postal votes, my invitation to join him had been "lost in the post" and mislaid by the Royal Mail, who were obviously too busy preparing to deliver millions of national election leaflets on behalf of the 4,500 PCs from all the parties.

Reform UK had chosen to set out their policies and launch a "crusade to defend British values" at the distinctly tatty-looking 'Gurnos Social Club' on a rundown housing estate in Merthyr Tydfil, "because it shows everyone exactly what happens to a country when Labour is in charge." NF called it a 'contract' with the British people, which was exciting and inventive as he explained that the word "manifesto" had been devalued-and was something which people associated with lies, broken promises, and failure to deliver. For those who recognised that "manifesto" was not some sort of exotic South American dish, the mere mention of the word usually led to polite yawns and people's eyes glazing over. However, I found that 'contract' was a simple but intelligent choice of word that struck a chord with people. It was much more personal, allowed me to look them in the eye, and was something that everyone understood. It resonated with them, and they found it descriptive in the same way as the name of the party because "it did what it said on the tin"-in a straightforward and no-nonsense way. So, I found it a useful marketing tool to have in the armoury and use in my sales pitch.

The contract included promises to cut income tax, leave the ECHR (European Convention on Human Rights), tax cuts of £88 billion, and scrapping the doomed to fail net zero targets to save £30bn. Although the IFS said the plans "don't add up" and would cost "tens of billions of pounds per year," it also addressed something that other parties were so reluctant to: freezing non-essential immigration. While the vote on Brexit and leaving the EU[30] resulted in a very close-run result, no voter on the continent went to the ballot box to open the floodgates to uncontrolled mass immigration of millions of unvetted immigrants. Here was a politician prepared to face the facts![31]

---

[30] *Brexit: Having joined the EC at the beginning of 1973, the UK became the only member state to withdraw from its successor, the EU, in January 2020 after a referendum was held.*

[31] *Examples of how badly broken Britain's immigration was would have been as laughable as they were ridiculous had they not been true: a Sudanese asylum seeker with a 'receding hairline and facial hair' being defined as a child by a judge, a drug dealer being allowed to remain in the country after promising to only smoke cannabis, a Sri Lankan sex offender being allowed to stay because he was gay).*

Farage was pragmatic and honest enough to admit that the party could not win the election this time around but stressed that this was about putting the party in the strongest possible position for 2029. This was something I would be able to parrot to people whenever I had the opportunity.

While Lord Cruddas, a Tory peer and former party donor, shared dozens of social media posts supportive of Farage and Reform UK, the polls continued to predict doom for the Conservatives. But Rishi appeared to be dreaming out loud when he claimed, "I believe we can win." This prompted the understatement of the campaign so far from Grant Shapps, the Defence Secretary, whose retort was that "it was not the most likely outcome."

Sunak scored another politically inept own goal and found himself in the middle of yet another furor when he pulled out of attending the glamorous annual Black & White Ball. This was a huge fundraising event for his party, at which supporters paid as much as £1,500 to attend and where the PM was traditionally the star guest.

Tuesday 18th June

Front pages:

Daily Express: BANKING GIANT'S DIRE WARNING ON LABOUR PLEDGES

The Times: Don't risk a generation of socialism, warn Tories

Daily Mail: RISHI: KEIR ONLY WANTS VOTES AT 16 TO 'ENTRENCH HIS POWER'

The Guardian: Farage accused of cut and spend manifesto 'that doesn't add up'

The Daily Telegraph: Tories turn to Johnson to counter Reform

i: Farage: It's 'impossible' to know if Reform would keep low-tax pledge

Today was the final day for people to register to vote and my long-awaited leaflets were finally delivered by a courier and, while they may have represented junk mail to many of their recipients, they were like gold dust to me. After a worryingly large quantity of extremely heavy cardboard boxes were unloaded directly from the courier's van into my ageing car and mobile HQ, I drove straight to Kettering to deliver them to the first group of people who'd been able to contact me via my personal email address and without whom I would have been completely lost.

On the journey, I recalled a survey I'd read which claimed that the average home received as many as 450 pieces of junk mail each year. As a householder myself, I was acutely aware that unsolicited mail was the bane of most people's lives, so I felt guilty that I was about to be responsible for adding to what I understood was an unwanted invasion of privacy for most recipients. In this day and age, leafleting seems an archaic way of communication and social media must surely be the most effective way into people's homes, although it occurred to me that unsolicited emails would probably contravene the dreaded GDPR restrictions. Anyway, social media doesn't provide the chance to meet voters face to face, which I was about to do.

Several people had kindly rallied around and volunteered to help me distribute them but, apart from some who had kindly signed my nomination forms, most of them hadn't met me. I had to be very targeted in where I leafleted and not only did I have to map out and coordinate strategic territories for distribution, but I also had to ensure that individuals were bona fide and not likely to sabotage my efforts by disposing of large quantities of leaflets in the nearest skip - and this was not the work of a moment.

The first drop-off was with a delightful retiree of South African descent called Randall, whom I had arranged to meet in the car park outside one of the cut-priced German supermarket chains. He was one of the first to offer to distribute some leaflets for me. Somehow it all seemed very clandestine: having arrived at the prescribed time, I searched for the ageing red Jeep Cherokee with a black bonnet that he had described to me for the 'handover'. A covert but entirely innocent meeting between two complete strangers in a supermarket car park felt slightly uncomfortable for some reason. As I passed over the large envelope stuffed with my personalised flyers, I was aware that it might even have looked suspiciously like a covert and illegal transaction between two middle aged men to anyone not in the know. However, after a good chat with my volunteer, I was unjustifiably relieved that I wasn't chased out of the supermarket car park by blaring sirens and blue flashing lights.

It turned out to be a stroke of luck that the first time I ventured outdoors (and feeling a little self-conscious) sporting one of my three precious Reform rosettes (two would have looked silly...) it was outside a supermarket. As I wandered around aimlessly searching for Randall's apparently distinctive but difficult-to-find car, it was noticeable how many strangers approached me and expressed their curiosity about the party. This was not only reassuring but taught me an early and very valuable lesson about where to find heavy footfall and a constant stream of people who were receptive to taking leaflets and sufficiently interested to stop and chat, but critically not for so long that they took up too much valuable time. Whether they were on the way in or out of the store, they were invariably and understandably in a hurry, especially if accompanied by impatient or bored children. Conversations were invariably short, factual, and to the point, so it proved to be an efficient use of time for all concerned.

I'm not entirely sure why this was as effective as it was, but I soon learnt that people appeared much more focused when visiting specialist shops to look at or buy a specific product, and as a result, they were less interested in talking than they were outside a supermarket where they were happier to delay the drudgery of their routine food shopping.

In much the same way I soon discovered that distributing leaflets at the railway station was not as 'lucrative', even though there was a lot of human traffic, because everyone was even more focused on either running for their trains in the morning or rushing back home in the evening and I needed to be sensitive to that.

The underfunded and overcrowded Kettering General Hospital was always busy, but hit and miss, as visitors understandably had other, more important things on their mind, even though the venue itself was a major subject of political debate. While the town centre and shopping malls obviously had high levels of footfall, it was outside the many supermarkets where volumes of people seemed most prepared to engage with me.

Distributing what looked like just a small handful of leaflets for Paul Hogan throughout my own village the previous day had proved to be very good practice for what I was to face, and gave me an insight into what appeared to be an easy task. It wasn't. A handful containing a couple of hundred A5 leaflets may not look a lot to deliver at first glance, but if you do it properly and as diligently as my unpaid volunteers all did for me, you soon realise how long it takes; it's remarkably time-consuming and extremely hard work. I had 20,000 of the wretched things to distribute, which would have been impossible on my own, and it was still a daunting task even with my team of tireless volunteers.

I quickly gained huge respect and newfound empathy for our conscientious "posties" and the hazards they contend with on a daily basis. Whilst they have the advantage of knowledge about their regular beats, I couldn't always find the right entrance or the correct door to post the said leaflet. easiest and ideal drops were into outside letterboxes, but the quality of Paul's missives was as bad and flimsy as mine would also prove to be when they eventually arrived. I soon learnt that it was not a simple job to get them through letterboxes, most of which had draft excluders that wouldn't allow a single piece of paper to be pushed through easily. When I tried to do so, they often ended up as a crumpled mess and so would be even less likely to be read by the recipient than the more commonly delivered piece of junk mail advertising plastic garden furniture or home improvements.

The worst letterboxes were those positioned at the bottom of people's front doors, which firstly meant bending down almost to one's hands and knees. This might have been good exercise but was an unwelcome addition for those like me with bad backs already exacerbated by being on one's feet all day. I can't think why anyone who devised this thought it was a good idea, but they obviously either had an odd sense of humour or just didn't like long-suffering postmen and women. This arrangement had the added disadvantage of being at dog level, so anyone poking their fingers through risked being bitten by a four-legged home 'security guard'!

I found it much safer and more satisfactory to be introduced to household pets in person rather than meeting them informally via fingers poking through a low-slung aperture which understandably they interpreted as an infringement of their territorial rights. I was fortunate that I only encountered a handful of canine 'Terrierists' and wasn't brave enough to find out whether their barks were really more vicious than their bites. I was concerned that if I suffered damage to my hands requiring bandaging, it would make the rest of my task near impossible and leave me even more reliant on other people.

The other excuse I allowed myself was that the possibility of appearing at the count on election night with both hands bandaged might have caused amusement for onlookers but probably wouldn't have projected quite the right image. So, the coward in me would try to find somewhere else to strategically slide my piece of paper under - out of the dog's way and in the hope that it would be seen by the homeowner before it was washed away by the reliably unreliable British weather.

The most embarrassing incident that occurred due to one of these ankle-high letterboxes was when my signet ring got caught on a particularly strong piece of rubber draft-excluding material and dropped onto the floor on the other side of the door. Fortunately, the homeowner was in and, alerted by the noise of her yapping dog which was trying to prevent me from retrieving it opened her front door to find me lying on my side, flustered and disheveled, grovelling around on her doorstep with my hand poking through her letterbox. Fortunately, once she realised I didn't represent a danger and hadn't been trying to break into her house, she saw the funny side. We had a brief chat before I continued my rounds, and she pledged to vote for me - but only after I autographed the offending item for her..!

Reflecting the view that people like me were just cannon fodder, we were all asked by his campaign manager (a concept that I could only dream about) if we could attend Ben Habib's day of action outside a hotel in Wellingborough. The promised media coverage might have been useful, but I declined as I had so much catching up to do and desperately needed to get out and be seen in my own “territory”.

I spent the rest of the day driving all over the constituency, distributing these irritating bits of paper to my enthusiastic band of volunteers, although I couldn’t help wondering how many of them would actually be looked at - let alone read - bearing in mind their naturally short ‘shelf life’.

Carole Shrigley and her partner Ian Blackwell became greatly valued allies and were a constant source of refreshments every time I dropped in to deliver yet another box of thousands of leaflets. Single-handedly, Ian delivered more than anyone else and always cheerfully offered to do so without question - even when we discovered that my logistical arrangements had gone awry and he was duplicating an area that had already been covered by someone else due to my poor sense of geography.

Circumstances continued to work against me and the various ongoing IT delays ensured that I still hadn’t been ‘GDPR’d’, even though I’d now attended the course. This meant that I wasn’t allowed to receive the regular press briefings, which would have been useful to say the least, and it didn’t please me that I didn’t have access to them when it was my job to market to people I’d never met and inspire them with confidence in both myself and the party.

With no sense of leadership from elsewhere in the region, let alone from ‘higher up’, I was still staggering around in the dark with very little sense of direction and virtually no guidance other than words of encouragement from Sean and the camaraderie and sharing of daily experiences with the other local PCs on the WhatsApp group, which at least kept my spirits up and ensured a degree of sanity.

***

Reform announced that they were threatening a vetting company with legal action, claiming they had been conned because, despite paying them £144,000 in April to warn them away from unsuitable PPCs who held offensive or unacceptable views, several were found to have posted extreme material online.

The company in question was the unimaginatively named ‘vetting.com’ (vetting.con?!) and *The Spectator* revealed that its parent company was co-owned by an ex-Tory advisor who had worked under Boris Johnson when he was in the driving seat as PM. Reform had been assured that there was no conflict of interest, but an angry NF blasted, “This is an establishment stitch-up. The owner of the vetting company has deep links to the Tory party and they have some serious questions to answer.”

The reality was that every party had the same problem in the rush to fill as many of the constituency seats as they were able to, and Reform had fewer PCs in place when Rishi dropped his bombshell announcement. In their quest to be taken seriously as a political party, Reform rushed to field as many candidates as possible and it was inevitable that some bad pennies slipped through the net.

Although I was not one of them and think I proved to be a help rather than a hindrance, the media bias against Reform was such that they made sure to give full scrutiny to any bad eggs in the Reform party but much less coverage to those like the Lib Dem candidate Alan Good, who had posted images on X showing he received work messages from constituents on the gay dating app Grindr.

Wednesday 19th June

Front pages:

Daily Express: PM: LABOUR WILL TAX YOUR YEARS OF SAVINGS IN WEEKS

Daily Mirror: TORIES ADRIFT FROM REALITY. YOU'RE GOING TO NEED A BIGGER VOTE

The Times: Starmer 'tax threat' to savers with a chequebook

The Guardian: NHS will buy beds in care homes to cut hospital waits, says Labour

Daily Mirror: LABOUR'S SECRET TAX RISE DOSSIER

Financial Times: Tory hopefuls jockey for position as post-poll race to succeed Sunak looms

The most obvious demographic and the 'low-hanging fruit' (a ghastly expression over used at every possible opportunity predominantly by American bankers) was long-term, if not lifelong, Tory voters over 60 who, like me, felt betrayed by the government of the last 14 years.

On the streets of Kettering and knocking on doors in outlying villages, I was aware that, to many people, I was nothing more than a door-to-door salesman. However, once the cynics realised that I wasn't trying to flog them double glazing or organic dog food, I was invariably made to feel a little more welcome and treated with both patience and courtesy - perhaps because they felt some sympathy for some of the tedium and necessary repetition involved in my role?!

Introducing 'lucky number seven' into my choreographed 'sales' patter, I made the point that we had the highest taxes in 70 years, the highest government spending in 70 years, and the highest national debt in 70 years. Also, that we had the longest NHS waiting lists in 70 years and we've had the lowest growth decade for 70 years. Everything - be it food, fuel or heating - costs a fortune and we have utterly uncontrolled immigration, both legal and illegal.

Either it wasn't a bad 'script' to use or I was just very convincing, as I encountered very few people who disagreed with me. I was interested to note how many households were divided in their views between Reform and other parties. However, in many cases, the majority of the latter were sufficiently engaged in my sales patter to compliment me on giving them something to think about. Many of my visits to households that were split in opinion actually ended with them saying I'd won them over and that I'd get their vote. I'll never know where they actually put the **X** come election day and whether they were just being polite and wanted me to leave them in peace, but positive reactions like this were encouraging anyway.

The Lib Dems may have been a sanctuary for the politically homeless, but throughout the course of my life they had always seemed completely pointless, with no strong views or clear policies on anything. Very middle of the road, in fact, but in the words of Nye Bevan[32] "We know what happens to people who stay in the middle of the road. They get run over." In no way could Reform ever be accused of being middle of the road. The party knows exactly which direction it's travelling in and is for people like me who truly care about the state of the nation, its history, and its culture. That should not be defined as extremism, merely as

---

[32] *Aneurin "Nye" Bevan was a Welsh Labour party MP who as Minister of Health pioneered the, creation of the NHS.*

recognition of our heritage and traditional British values by people who want them restored.

I feel very strongly that this country is our home, and should not be viewed as an all-expenses-paid hotel. However charitable and hospitable we may be as a nation, an annual influx of almost one million net immigrants is completely unacceptable. More importantly and it's hardly rocket science. this is economically unsustainable, especially when we are completely failing to look after our own people, witnessed by the fact that the streets of our towns and cities are increasingly filled with homeless people. What is worse is that many of those whom our society has turned its back on are ex-servicemen who have previously protected our borders, without which we don't have a country.

The current Conservative MP was Philip Hollobone, who had been in situ for 19 years and was described as being many things by many people. He was very low profile and I had never even heard of him, nor at that point met him, so I couldn't comment or sympathise with them. However, the consensus was that he was an extremely dull character, lacking in and devoid of any charisma. Wikipedia quotes him as saying that his job is to "represent constituents in Westminster, it's not to represent Westminster in the constituency". If that were the case, I rather liked and respected the sentiment, and a lot of Tory and Reform voters told me that he had actually been a good MP who was on top of local issues.

Like me, he'd also had a lengthy career in the City and so neither of us were "twelve-year-olds", as one voter described some of the other candidates in the constituency! As with police officers who seem to get younger by the day, it was also true of the candidates vying to become MPs. Certainly, the age and lack of 'life' and business experience was a concern aired by many across all ages, and not just the older generation of voters.

I was well aware that my 30-year professional career as a banker might not endear me to voters, as it was right up there with the most hated and least respected occupations such as estate agents, family lawyers, and car salesmen. Yet here I was, immersing myself into the universally disliked role of politician. If I had a USP at all, it was that, despite being a privately educated ex-City boy with a middle-class accent and an inconvenient name, I resonated with voters in contrast to many other PCs and was of a 'certain age' - although a lot of the younger generation resent the relative fortune that 'baby boomers' like me have benefitted from.

I had been short of hair since my late twenties but now I was a balding, white, middle-aged man (aka pale and male but definitely not stale...), something that might also have worked against me, but strangely it didn't seem to. At the end of the day, people want the best candidates and people for the job irrespective of sex, colour, or background, and they wanted someone to represent their best interests and whom they could trust. For many people, telling them that "I'm a politician and an honest person" puts them off straight away and is analogous to someone saying either that they're a prostitute but a virgin or a fox telling a field full of lambs that he'd go vegetarian were he to be elected...

The Labour Party historically is full of MPs who are so-called career politicians, which is really just a euphemism for people who have either worked only for the trade unions or in the public sector. People warmed to the fact that I was very obviously not a career politician and hadn't been involved with politics even at a local level, nor had I ever had the remotest aspiration of being an MP. To my surprise, that seemed to make me more attractive to the electorate, who had lost complete trust in the political class and wanted someone who could relate with them.

As already mentioned, there are no qualifications to being one, but being over 60 years old meant that not only had I been in business, but also that I'd had a few decades of real-life experience, which they liked - and this seemed to win me both credibility and respect from a lot of the electorate whom I met.

As expected, I ticked some boxes with the older, traditionally Tory demographic but was also able to connect with many of the middle-aged group that I still felt I emotionally belonged to. Maybe because my sons were both in their mid-twenties, I was able to relate to - and even gain some traction with - their cohort as well, although this was the most difficult demographic to engage with and the least likely to bother to vote.

***

Inflation fell to the Bank of England's target of 2%, the lowest level in almost three years, thus showing signs of turning a corner whilst also reinforcing the view that Rishi had called the election too early.

Inflation wasn't the only thing falling, though, as the latest YouGov poll reiterated that the government's popularity was continuing to do so as well. As election fever mounted, the latest YouGov poll suggested that Labour would secure 425 seats, the Tories 108, the Liberal Democrats 67, Reform UK five, and the SNP 20 - which, apart from the latter, was reasonably prophetic.

The Sun quoted Lord Frost as saying that the Tories would be doing better under Johnson; however, Boris was expected to skip election campaigning to go on his second summer holiday to celebrate his 60th birthday within the next few days, and wasn't likely to return to the UK until the day before voters go to the polls.

Labour suspended one of its candidates, Andy Brown, who is standing in Aberdeenshire North and Moray East, after reports he shared "pro-Russian" material online which he denied.

Thursday 20th June

Front pages:

The Daily Telegraph: Tory wipeout

The Guardian: Reeves pledges to close gender pay gap 'once and for all' if Labour wins

The Times: Tories set to suffer worst poll defeat for 100 years

The Independent: Major poll shock: Sunak to lose seat in Tory bloodbath

Financial Times: Sunak claims credit as inflation hits BoE's target for first time in 3 years

i: Tories despair as poll signals worst defeat in 200 years

Sam Wildman's article appeared in the hard copy print version of *The Northants Telegraph* with the same strapline as the online version, which had appeared a week earlier, quoting me from the press release saying: "I'm the voice of common sense." I had no idea of the number of hits per week that the online version would get, but the weekly circulation of the hard copy newspaper was about 4,400, and I banked on the fact that each copy would be read by at least one member of each household-hopefully rather more. It was therefore extremely important and one of the few weapons in my otherwise negligible armoury.

The gist of the article was that people are fed up with the cost of living, having no money, failing public services and endless broken promises, and that Reform UK are the only party that really want to fix this. I hoped that, as we go to the polls, they wouldn't tick the boxes for the same tired old MPs who fail them year after year, but that they would have the courage to do something different by voting for change and Reform.

The article on me only took up a quarter of a page, but whether by design or coincidence, the editorial department chose to place it on the same page as an advertisement that my significantly better-funded fellow Reform candidate, Ben Habib, had taken out, which occupied the half-page below my article. This was very fortuitous, as my ex-wife had left me with insufficient means to afford an advertising campaign of my own, so by default I was, in effect, piggybacking on Ben-who, after all, was expounding exactly the same party line as me. I had every reason to be thankful to Ben for unwittingly assisting my cause and, as a well-known supermarket chain whose stores I spent so much time standing outside says in its slogan, “every little helps”!

After an unacceptable series of interminable delays, I had finally been given access to my Reform constituency email address, which brought with it an inbox overflowing with a backlog of thousands of unanswered emails. This included one from several weeks ago from the Rector of Kettering, who was chairing a hustings for the constituency tonight, to which I’d been invited. However, with only a few hours' notice, I was unable to attend due to a longstanding prior commitment elsewhere in the constituency that couldn’t be cancelled. Otherwise, I would have welcomed the opportunity to go to what was to be the only hustings I was invited to.

Hustings are an effective way for voters to make direct comparisons between individual politicians and their party policies under one roof but can be of limited benefit to PCs, as they’re often attended by people who want to disrupt, discredit and set them up for a fall. I later received several messages of abuse for not attending but felt there was no substitute for getting out and about, talking to the ordinary man in the street, so it was a case of ‘mixed blessings’ that I was unable to make it.

I was surprised at the paucity of hustings generally, and whilst my Northamptonshire colleagues and I were all keen to accept any invitations, it was clear that some candidates from other parties had been spooked and declined due to fears about their personal safety. This had led to some events being cancelled altogether.

One of the more intriguing emails I received that day was from Northamptonshire Police, which showed photos of curiously wrapped and unsolicited packages that some PCs had been sent by marketing companies. Although I would have welcomed new additions to my wardrobe or tickets to sporting events and concerts as so many Labour politicians were given, I was to be disappointed; these packages were entirely innocent as they only contained the not quite so glamorous freebies such as notebooks, pens, stickers and other promotional election paraphernalia. In the absence of receiving anything similar from the party itself, I was sure I could have used some of the contents and waited for my delivery with much anticipation but I was either not deemed to be important enough or sufficiently deserving. Alternatively it had been lost in the post together with myriads of postal votes, by the inefficient and overpriced mail service that we have in this country because mine never arrived. Although I was gutted, at least I could never be accused of accepting inducements!

***

The Labour Party has always shown a woeful lack of understanding about the countryside, which they seem to view as a giant theme park full of Nimbys[33], and about the importance of the rural farmers who put food on our tables. It was for good reason that one of the many soubriquets that the future PM would acquire was 'Starmer the Farmer Harmer'.

Today, NF made a surprise visit to Ormskirk in rural Lancashire where, showing rather greater respect and empathy for the industry than his Labour counterpart, he promoted his agenda of support for local farmers. He was also supporting a local PC in the seaside town of Blackpool, where he was speaking at the town's Imperial Hotel and claimed he had been proven "right to use the word invasion" to describe a group of children and adults getting out of a dinghy on a beach in Kent in 2020. He admitted: "I used a very naughty word, an unforgivable word. I said this would lead to an invasion," he told the crowd. "You would have thought I'd advocated killing the first-born..."

He was noticeably absent on BBC TV's *Question Time* "leaders' special" despite his repeated demands that he be included in the line-up.

---

[33] *Nimby is an acronym for "Not In My Back Yard"*

Friday 21st June

Front pages:

The Daily Telegraph: Starmer: Corbyn better than Johnson as PM

Daily Mirror: TORY BETTING SCANDAL. WHAT ARE THE ODDS ON THAT?

The Guardian: New blow for PM as former Tory minister says he will vote Labour

The Times: Sunak vows to boot out Tories over poll betting

Daily Mail: CORBYN WOULD HAVE BEEN BETTER PM THAN BORIS, KEIR CLAIMS

i: Betting farce derails Tory campaign amid fears that more names will emerge

Financial Times: Flurry of bets on July election placed in run-up to Sunak's announcement

The Independent: All bets off on trust in Tories

Metro: WHAT A FLUTTER SHAMBLES

My Facebook page was now generating some traffic, most of which was positive, but inevitably there were some keyboard warriors who had too much time on their hands and were hell-bent on making trouble and discrediting me. I could have done without the unnecessary distraction but refused to get drawn into a spat with a pair of them, clearly working in cahoots with each other and either unsubtly trying to discredit me and/or totally unaware that, like many of the party PCs, apart from my loyal band of leafleteers, I was completely on my own-knocking on doors, speaking to groups in public, and posting, to the limit of my ability, on social media. It simply wasn't possible to be in all the places I would like to have been at the same time.

One correspondent berated me for being absent from the previous evening's hustings and failing to "show my face", to which I responded that it was not due to any lack of commitment but because I had not had access to the elusive Kettering email address until very recently and only received the invitation a few hours before the hustings actually took place. By then, I was otherwise occupied elsewhere. I would have welcomed the opportunity to meet another large group of people, but "Alex" wasn't satisfied with my explanation and complained that he hadn't seen any social media or other coverage of my "alternative appointments".

I offered my (in)sincere apologies that he didn't have access to my diary but imagined he was an example of a disruptive saboteur, or an ill-informed lager-lout who had turned up to make trouble and was irritated that I hadn't been there to spar with. However, twenty-seven years of marriage to my former wife had taught me to be very selective in terms of choosing which battles were worth fighting, and I concluded that this wasn't one to waste time on. It was probably just as well for this pest that I hadn't been there in person, as the provocative tone in which he communicated was such that he might have benefited from a John Prescott-style punch on the nose![34] Others accused Reform of having "policies which didn't have any basis in fact" and of "spouting division and hate", none of which was true.

I didn't know how to "tweet" and I'm not on Instagram, so I was aware that my low profile on social media would work against me. Whilst I'm fairly thick-skinned, some of the abuse I received was a reminder that it is a double-edged sword, and I was sometimes grateful that I didn't have a higher presence on it. The modern world now expects and has become used to the instant gratification that it provides, and whilst it offers a very effective medium to reach out to large swathes of people and potentially garner support, thanks to faceless and often anonymous cowards using it as a medium to bully and harass others, it can also be a scary

---

[34] *John Prescott was the colourful Labour MP and who was hit in face with an egg thrown by a protestor on the day that the Labour manifesto had been launched for the 2001 General election, Also known as 'Two Jags' due to his ownership of (more than one) Jaguar, the Deputy PM was also dubbed 'Two jabs' having punched his assailant in the face in an act of what he claimed to be self defense.*

place. I became inured to it and learnt not to take online abuse too much to heart, on the basis that it came from anonymous trolls who had never actually met me, so reasoned that their comments couldn't actually be that personal.

That evening, Juliet and I took a welcome break from campaigning to join my sons and their friends in London to celebrate my eldest son's engagement to his lovely fiancée.

***

Nigel ensured that he remained in the forefront of the news when, speaking to Nick Robinson on the BBC TV *Panorama* programme, he said he'd been warning about conflict with Russia since 2014 when he stood up in the European Parliament and said there would be a war in Ukraine, and that it was a direct consequence of the ever eastward expansion of NATO and the European Union, which had given Vladimir Putin a reason to tell the Russian people that "they're coming for us again" and to go to war. The conflict is Putin's fault, he said, but "we've provoked this war".

Separately, he claimed that Ofcom were engaging in election interference and that their new rules would only allocate Reform UK 8% of the coverage, saying they were trying to protect the cosy establishment from new challengers like us.

Of more local interest, Nick Adderley, the Chief Constable of Northamptonshire Police, was dismissed without notice for gross misconduct and placed on the police barred list by an internal panel, which upheld all allegations against him and said that he had “built a military naval legend that wasn’t true”. Apparently, he implied that he had served in the Falklands War, despite being only 15 years old when the conflict began in 1982, and he didn’t embark for the Falklands until after the hostilities had actually ended.

In a move of which our future Chancellor would have been proud, he claimed on his CV that he had been in the Royal Navy for ten years, when he had served for only two. He had also lied about attending the prestigious Britannia Royal Naval College for four years, despite having his application rejected. Furthermore, he falsely claimed to have seen active service during his naval career, to have been a military negotiator in Haiti (despite never visiting the country), and to have been a “commander or a lieutenant”, even though he only achieved the rank of able seaman. It was not a good look and suggested that the vetting process he’d been through had been even worse than the screening of candidates by political parties. The reputational damage it did to the local police force was unquantifiable, and the loss in confidence was evident from many of the conversations I had with people on my travels. Adderley said that one of the most painful aspects of the case was “the hurt that I have caused to veterans of the armed forces… as I come from a very proud family of veterans”, but no one could be quite sure whether that was another fabrication of his fertile imagination.

I had come into contact with the alleged fraudster at the beginning of his tenure when we were both guests at a dinner hosted by the High Sheriff of Northamptonshire, and found him good company and very plausible. I remember being surprised when he told me what a problem immigrants were in Northampton. Despite being landlocked, the town is close to the point where the M1 motorway intersects with the A14, and he said that each Tuesday night the police force had to cope with an influx of young men who needed food and housing, having illegally entered the country via Harwich hidden in articulated trucks, from which they alighted once the vehicles stopped overnight at the local lorry parks.

I subsequently contacted him several times about the investment made by his force in the proliferation of revenue-earning mobile speed camera vans, which were deliberately and cynically placed to earn maximum profits instead of being situated in accident black spots. He never responded; maybe because he was too busy polishing the fake medals that he had ‘acquired’ during the Falklands War.

Saturday 22nd June

Front pages:

The Daily Telegraph: Starmer will reverse Brexit, says Badenoch

Daily Mail: FARAGE: THE WEST 'PROVOKED' PUTIN

The Times: JK Rowling: Labour has turned its back on women

Even though I had now travelled to and from Kettering many times, I have never possessed any sense of direction – hence why I've always competed in old cars on race circuits, where one goes around and around in 'circles' in the same direction and without the need of a map, so at least I can be sure that I'm unlikely to get lost. As a result, I needed a car with a good navigation system to make the daily journey to, and in and around, the constituency, so I chose my ageing Porsche Macan as my "Battle Bus". It was equipped with a reliable satnav, was more practical and less ostentatious than my other cars, and was the only one I possessed that had more than two doors.

It had been the family car and was one of the few possessions that I had managed to reclaim from the divorce, but I was concerned that it might not present the right image to constituents and potential voters. Although an ordinary-looking hatchback SUV, it was still a Porsche, which had its brand emblazoned in large letters on its rump. I made a feeble attempt to tape over the offending branding with some black insulating tape, which must have been made somewhere in Asia because, by the time of my first stop, it had come unstuck and fluttered away on the motorway.

Whilst there was nothing I could do about that, I did arrange for the DVLA to replace the personal registration plate with an age-related and anonymous number, which I felt would be a better look. In my attempts not to flaunt the car, I was always careful to park it out of sight of the houses and people I visited on my daily rounds, but there were inevitably a few who spotted it and made comments on the lines of how I was "alright then", implying that I had no need to worry about finances. If only they'd known the truth, but the dialogue wasn't about me, and the cost of living crisis would prove to be a major source of concern for everyone I spoke to.

However, it was not the first time I was made to feel embarrassed and even slightly guilty about owning something that might be misconstrued as displaying a modicum of success from the modest wealth that I'd earned and been able to retain from the grasping hands and iniquities of the family law courts.

Before I set off to what was almost becoming my second home, I attended to a flurry of emails and messages on Facebook from people complaining that they hadn't received any leaflets. If I'd had more time, I like to think that I could have organised deliveries by my faithful team of volunteers with near military precision, but given the time constraints imposed on me by the party's inefficiencies and despite their best efforts there were inevitably a few areas that were missed entirely.

In theory, every household should also have received a generic version from the party, which also had my name and photo on it, but the machinations of Royal Mail were such that many of those didn't reach people either. The dialogue at least encouraged some more offers of help from additional volunteers.

Of more significance were the angry messages and inevitable backlash over NF's remarks about Putin and Ukraine, and this continued in some of my face-to-face skirmishes in town. I was accosted by an unpleasant character of indeterminate age who had just stumbled out of a pub, where he'd clearly spent most of the afternoon and, somewhat worse for wear, accused me of being a Nazi fascist.

Less aggressive but just as bewildering was the reaction from a (sober) and much older lady who told me, "Oh, I couldn't vote for Reform, too right-wing, 1930s Germany and all that. Which is a shame as you look really normal." I took that as a compliment, as she obviously hadn't seen the photos of me on either my leaflet or the party website which, thanks to my sons' hurried photographic attempts, did not make me look at all normal.

Reform UK's election campaign had been going better than any of us could have hoped for at that point but, even though what Nigel had said made a lot of sense, the uncomfortable truth was that his comments were untimely and didn't help us at a critical stage in our campaign. That said, apart from the nameless wimps who posted unflattering comments on social media, I found the vast majority of people I engaged with – especially those in person – were very respectful, even those with whom we agreed to disagree. If that was unusual, maybe it was just a reflection of the natural good nature of the number of fine people I met in and around Kettering.

***

Both Starmer and Sunak condemned Nigel for his claim. The PM said he was "completely wrong and only plays into Putin's hands", while Starmer called the remarks "disgraceful" and said anyone standing for Parliament should make clear Russia is the aggressor.

Farage, meanwhile, stirred it up by reiterating his stance and insisted he would not apologise for his remarks, but said that he was not an "apologist or supporter of Putin". He added, "I said I disliked him as a person, but I admired him as a political operator because he's managed to take control of running Russia."

NF was also busy tweeting on Twitter, where he accused Google of blocking the party's adverts in an attempt to stop the Reform message. Meanwhile, the Tories were again in the spotlight over the scandal of alleged betting on the election date, in which *The Independent* said Rishi Sunak failed to deny cabinet members were involved.

To add to the PM's woes, *The Daily Star* highlighted a poll which embarrassingly put Count Binface[35] only just behind the Prime Minister in his Yorkshire constituency of Richmond and Northallerton.

The Daily Telegraph focused on an interview with Business Secretary Kemi Badenoch, who warned that Labour will reverse Brexit if they win the General Election.

---

[35] *'Count Binface' aka comedian Jon Harvey stood as a candidate contesting the same seat as Rishi Sunak wearing his signature headgear that resembled a rubbish bin*

Sunday 23rd June

Front pages:

Sunday Express: LABOUR'S £2BN BLACK HOLE

The Sunday Telegraph: Handouts lack the dignity of wages, says Starmer

Sunday Mirror: THE RISHI GET RICHER as the poor get poorer

The Sunday Times: Top Tory 'placed dozens of bets on election date'

The Mail on Sunday: ZELENSKY: FARAGE IS INFECTED WITH 'VIRUS OF PUTIN'

The Observer: Starmer's growth plan 'doomed' without access to EU Markets

The Independent: The great turn-off... 40 per cent of young won't vote

It's debatable as to whether new MPs should have some form of training before they start working in public life and take on the huge responsibility of representing an average of 73,000 constituents, but history suggests that the vast majority of them would benefit enormously from doing so. In the same way, before they throw their hat in the ring to become a PPC, it would be sensible if individuals like me were given some guidance as to how to conduct an election campaign which, with the constraints on both time and resources, Reform UK simply weren't in a position to offer.

There are no formal qualifications required to put yourself forward and, of the 4,500 candidates, very few of the new ones will have all the attributes needed or have had experience of dealing with the media, debate, harassment and intimidation. A large part of the role involves sales and marketing: selling yourself to win the trust and confidence of voters, and marketing your party and its policies.

My experience of marketing sponsorship deals to companies to fund my teenage motor racing habit was followed by a 30-year career with investment banks in the City of London, which involved both the management of teams of people and the high-level selling of large shareholdings in companies and financial derivatives to other financial institutions. This stood me in good stead, so I felt relatively well-equipped with some of the requisite skills.

As well as being a champion of the cause, I definitely saw my role as an ambassador and salesman for the party, its strategy, proposals and vision, encapsulated in the "Contract" which we were offering the unsuspecting and sometimes sceptical voters in my constituency. There was an overwhelming sense in the country that too many politicians fell into the camp of 'Not aware... Don't care', and

I was determined to contradict that and demonstrate to people that I was aware and did care. I knew that before attempting to sell any product or concept to anybody, you need to know what they may or may not want and need, and that is as true in politics as in any form of business. As a Parliamentary Candidate this meant listening to people's concerns and wish lists, however unrealistic some of them might be.

Knocking on doors was extremely time-consuming and not an effective use of the limited time that Reform UK's machinations had left me. If the door was opened by someone who wanted to talk, I had to give them the time to offload their gripes and concerns, although often the only way that some people were able to articulate these was to recount, at least part of their life story. It was touching that so many were prepared to share details of their personal circumstances with someone they'd never met before; sometimes I felt like a social worker.

This added to the realisation of the burden of responsibility that an MP has to be prepared to deal with and provided an interesting insight into the hard work and dedication required to be a credible MP. In this respect, I believe that the majority of people in this country who strive to become MPs, initially at least, go into politics for the right reasons - because they want to make a difference and genuinely believe that they can.

From a time management perspective, it was fortunate for me that not everyone did open their door, but for those who did, I had to limit the time I spent on the doorstep and make my apologies for moving on without being discourteous, and I became well-practised at doing so. No two conversations were quite the same, which could be both challenging and refreshing at the same time, and many people expressed their displeasure about the parlous state of the country and those who were governing it so badly in no uncertain terms.

There were specific local issues, of course, but the bigger picture was about the widespread dissatisfaction with the current government, the cost of living crisis, and the pound in their pocket (always central in any election), followed by the strain on our infrastructure: jobs, housing, the NHS, schools, roads, transport, and crime. It didn't need me to point the finger at immigration, but this was the common denominator that almost every single person I engaged with - whether in a group or individually - identified and blamed for their dissatisfaction with the way the country was being mismanaged and governed.

Whether it was not being able to get a GP appointment, overcrowded schools, lack of suitable housing, or the traffic levels in their neighbourhoods being unrecognisable from the levels of only five years ago, people were concerned and even frightened about the ramifications of the uncontrolled and unsustainable population explosion which they perceived to be the biggest single problem and the cause of falling economic growth. Everyone was feeling poorer as a result and were also genuinely uncomfortable with the proliferation of alien cultures and not hearing English voices in so many places that they no longer felt at home in their own country.

The good people of Kettering provided me with two memorable quotes which resonated with me and both of which were repeated on a fairly regular basis, so I wondered who had initiated them. Firstly, in comparing Labour and Conservative as "like two butt cheeks with little to choose between them", and secondly, an analogy on the unsustainable level of immigration, along the lines that: "If your bathtub was overflowing, then surely the first thing to do is not just to reach for the mop, but to turn off the tap immediately."

Whether it was leafleting, door-knocking, running street stalls, or speaking to local residents, there was always something to do, and that included dealing with a huge amount of correspondence. Less personal contact would be made through the party's constituency email address, where questions could often be answered with a one-line response, but in instances where this might seem too short, uncaring or abrupt, I took more time and effort with my replies to some of the essays that I received. This sometimes made me feel a bit like an agony aunt.

***

Further embarrassment for the Conservatives arose when *The Sunday Times* reported that a fourth senior Conservative was being investigated by the Gambling Commission over bets placed on the date of the election. Nick Mason, the party's chief data officer, allegedly placed multiple bets which the paper said could have generated thousands of pounds in winnings.

In response to this, the Labour Party campaign coordinator demanded that the Commission release the names of anyone else involved in the scandal so that people were aware of all the facts before they cast their votes.

Monday 24th June

Front pages:

Daily Express: RISHI: STARMER WILL UNPICK BREXIT AND REJOIN EU BY BACK DOOR

The Independent: Tories turn on MP over failure to get a grip on bet scandal

The Times: Labour plan for changing gender with less evidence

The Guardian: Sunak urged to drop candidates as betting investigation widens

Daily Mail: TEN DAYS TO STOP 'DISASTER' OF A STARMER SUPERMAJORITY

i: Tories question Sunak's leadership as he resists calls to suspend betting scandal suspects

Financial Times: Conservatives lose a third of their voters since January, survey finds

The Daily Telegraph: Labour to rip up school trans ban

Very few constituents asked me, or were remotely interested in or concerned about, where I lived, but most of those who did take an interest had no issue with the fact that I didn't live within the boundaries of the Kettering constituency. There's no actual requirement to live locally at all, and I was surprised to learn that an MP could even live outside the UK, which seems a ridiculous anomaly. Had I been elected, of course, I would have taken up residency in the constituency. Whilst it may not be ideal, it is quite common to find MPs representing an area different from where they live; in the same way that neither of our highest-profile candidates, Nigel Farage and Richard Tice, lived in

Essex or Lincolnshire respectively - nor did the soon to be outgoing, PM Rishi Sunak live in Yorkshire!

There were a few boringly predictable comments from some, mainly online, suggesting I wasn't as credible as several of the other candidates against whom I was competing, who, in fairness, did live in the constituency. I had some sympathy for their view that those candidates were more likely to be plugged into and attuned to local issues and sensitivities, which was true to a certain degree. However, it wasn't as though I was an alien from another planet (although the aforementioned publicity shots might have given a different impression...) and at least I had lived in the same county of Northamptonshire for thirty years. Of course, there was commonality of issues across the local constituencies.

Less valid were the more pointed and personal remarks from pathetic 'keyboard warriors' who retained their anonymity by posting under pseudonyms. One in particular said he/she had googled me, "knew where I lived" and had "discovered" that I lived in a Manor House which wasn't necessarily threatening but was quite spooky nonetheless. Of course, it was his/her/its (I'm not sure what sex should be 'assigned' to a troll or what pronouns they choose to masquerade under) right to do so, but they also questioned what qualifications I had to be an MP, having "only" worked in financial services.

The dialogue with this individual was clearly borne of 'green-eyed monster' jealousy and, had they bothered to make a more diligent search, they might have found something of greater relevance to satisfy their concerns. Wealth and aspiration are dirty words to some, but there is nothing wrong with harbouring those hopes and ambitions, and in the real world outside socialism, that is why so many millions play and dream of winning the lottery each week.

A rhinoceros-like skin is a prerequisite to cope with the occasional agitator, but having fought against the iniquity and unfairness of divorce law, together with the fabrications of my ex-wife and her lawyers, I was inured to this sort of thing and a bit of online abuse was like water off a duck's back. In any case, I was confident that these kinds of trolls were unlikely to vote for someone like me or for the party, so I was quick to close down any further communication. There was no merit in wasting time by pointing out to them that I'd come to this very late and, as a one-man band with limited resources and even less time to make up ground, it wasn't their problem - and neither were they interested in excuses.

One of my Reform colleagues went to a hustings in the neighbouring constituency of Corby, which was also attended by an Independent and both the Conservative, and the Lib Dem candidates. Notable by his absence that afternoon was any representation from Labour, whose candidate claimed that he couldn't make it because he'd be in Kettering for Keir Starmer's visit although the Conservative MP called his bluff by pointing out that this had actually taken place in the morning! Needless to say, even the Labour diehards were unimpressed with his no-show.

Although I saw no evidence of Starmer anywhere in my 'territory', I made sure that I was out and about in the centre of town, just in case he emerged and his presence led to an increase in footfall on the streets (it didn't seem to). I busied myself engaging with as many people as I could in the streets and shopping malls and was determined to be a distraction in the event that he appeared anywhere and was disappointed that we didn't appear in the same place at the same time.

Not surprisingly, the volume of phone calls I received over the course of these few weeks had increased enormously, which meant having my phone necessarily close at hand at all times. However, it also meant that the scourge of me making 'pocket calls' grew exponentially and became a daily occurrence of monotonous regularity, amusement and sometimes irritation for family and friends, who often found themselves on the receiving end of unwanted and sometimes lengthy voicemails containing either Radio 4 being broadcast from the car or, more often, me in full flow of conversation with a voter as I sat on or leant against my wretched phone for the countless time.

***

Speaking to ITV on their *Tonight* programme - and not understanding the effect that his comments on the subject were having in my constituency and no doubt many others - our leader again repeated his mantra on Ukraine when he said that the West had "provoked Putin stupidly". Although he supported giving munitions and help to the beleaguered country, he called for "sensible peace negotiations" with Putin to try and end the war with Russia.

He also held a last-minute rally in a car park in Newton Abbot, to a sell-out crowd of 1,500 people this evening, and was met by a standing ovation as he walked onto the stage, declaring the support "amazing". However, he called former PM Boris Johnson "morally repugnant" during the event and accused him of "hypocrisy", brandishing a copy of the *i* newspaper front page from 2016 that read "Boris blames EU for war in Ukraine".

Tuesday 25th June

Front pages:

The Times: Conversion therapy to be banned by Labour

The Daily Telegraph: Scotland Yard 'leaked names' in Tory betting scandal

Financial Times: Tory and Labour pledges to improve public services 'essentially underfunded'

i: Tories and Labour refuse to rule out 110 tax rises as IFS urges leaders to come clean

Before setting off to my 'patch', I dealt with emails ahead of a telephone interview with Sam at the *Northants Telegraph*.

Not all the emails and social media correspondence that I received were unpleasant; there were a lot of complimentary and uplifting messages of support too. One of the more charming communications I had was from someone professing to be a young "Student of Politics" based in Bournemouth, asking me to send one of my leaflets and even offering to pay for the postage, as he explained that he was trying to collect as many different ones as he could. Each to their own and after all lots of people like to collect strange things avidly, whether it be beer mats, stamps, coins, books, beer bottle tops, or, in my case, model racing cars. However, I'd never heard of anyone who collects parliamentary candidates' leaflets until then! The email was written in such a charming and enthusiastic way - and I enjoy compliments as much as anyone - so of course I replied that I would do so. In fact, I did better than that and sent him all those I'd received at home as a voter myself (although I first had to fish them out of my wheelie bin), together with those of some of my Reform colleagues, as well as examples I'd acquired from the candidates I was competing against in Kettering.

Instead of just sending him mine, I was pleased to add over 20 more to his collection and wondered not only how many he received in total but, more importantly, what he actually did with them. If they were anything like my cheaply produced product, they'd be good for recycling as low-quality loo paper. I should have asked him a bit more about his interest and wondered whether this was the beginning of a new craze in which people actually trade them like Pokémon cards, and if so, whether I could tap into the market, recoup some of the printing costs, and make money by selling some of those I would inevitably still have left over. I had visions of rare autographed copies selling at a huge premium. Maybe not..!

Several youngsters wrote in volunteering to help with the distribution of leaflets, which I was heartened by, but as PCs are not allowed to pay people to do this, I declined their generous offers, as I wanted to avoid potential accusations about unpaid 'child slavery'. A handful of teenagers also wrote in to ask if they could come and work with me in the Reform Party office once I had won the seat - an unrealistically optimistic but very flattering suggestion.

The young daughter of another constituent, who was one of my leafleting volunteers, said she'd help her father but only on condition that she could have one of my three remaining party rosettes to put on her bedroom wall alongside other examples she'd won in pony club events.

A huge amount of correspondence came from groups of tiresome lobbyists on a variety of issues, some local - which I always did my best to respond to - but mainly national issues. These were monotonous, time-wasting, repetitive in the extreme, often duplicated and uncoordinated in their approach.

Some of these subjects were also covered by individuals who asked leading questions regarding my views on issues like religion, abortion and assisted dying. My response to the latter was that in certain circumstances this should be viewed as shortening death rather than shortening life, which went down badly with one elderly lady who said she couldn't vote for me and would be voting for Labour instead. I refrained from pointing out to her that if a Starmer-led government carried out their plans to scrap the winter fuel allowance for the elderly, their policy would, in effect, be an endorsement of assisted dying. As the saying goes, you may please some of the people some of the time, but you can never please all of the people all of the time - and I sensed that, irrespective of the answer I gave some of the respondents, they wouldn't be putting their X in the box next to my name anyway!

***

A great story was that Labour deemed it necessary to suspend Kevin Craig as a candidate for Central Suffolk and North Ipswich after it emerged that the Gambling Commission had launched an investigation into a bet he had placed on himself losing in his constituency. Betting on your job doesn't always go to plan, but he was subsequently cleared of any offence.

Perhaps there was something in the name Craig, because despite knowing about the issue for almost two weeks, Sunak finally also announced that he was suspending Craig Williams.

The issue of the Prime Minister's PPS placing a £100 bet three days prior to the announcement of the date of the election had been rumbling on for days and had been referred to the Gambling Commission to determine whether Williams had placed the bet based on confidential information, to gain an advantage, which would amount to cheating under the Gambling Act and could constitute a criminal offence.

It became part of a wider scandal involving other members of the Conservatives, including Laura Saunders, their candidate for Bristol North West, who is married to the party's head of campaigning, Tony Lee who'd already taken leave of absence. It left a bad taste in the mouth and forced the party to announce that they'd withdrawn support for them and that, in the event they were elected, they would not be granted the whip.

Presumably, Sunak chose to do this today in the vain hope that the bad news would be buried by Labour's own predicament and detract from his own. But it wasn't.

Secretary of State for Scotland and Cabinet minister Alister Jack was the latest figure to become embroiled in the scandal after he claimed that he'd won £2,000 by betting on the timing of the election but insisted that he had not broken any watchdog rules.

Coming from an industry where insider trading is obviously not tolerated, I was surprised to learn that it's not actually illegal for politicians to bet on the outcome of elections (provided they aren't using inside information). However, I felt strongly that there was a conflict of interest in doing so. Besides, this was not a sporting event, candidates were not racehorses and were there to do a serious job. It's hardly big business, with only £450,000 placed on political bets compared to over £300 million on the Grand National each year. But even so, as Williams had clearly taken a big risk in placing one, bearing in mind his position, my criminal mind wondered why, firstly, he hadn't asked someone else to go to the bookies on his behalf, and secondly, why he didn't do so for more than £100! As I mentioned before, I'm not into betting, but if I were tempted to bet on anything in politics, it would only be on how long it would be before Chancellor-in-waiting Rachel Reeves got found out and would last in her job!

I faced yet more flack both online and on the streets today when defending Nigel's comments on Ukraine. I explained that they had been taken out of context and reiterated that it was something he had "predicted" 10 years ago when he said that NATO and the EU risked provoking a Russia that does not view Western intentions as benign. I repeated the party line that we thought Putin's invasion was immoral, outrageous, as well as indefensible and illegal. I also emphasised that NF was neither a supporter nor an apologist for Putin. This seemed to appease most of those who brought up the subject, so I was relieved and more comfortable when conversations moved on from this unwanted distraction to subjects which included some of my pet topics, which I felt were of more immediate importance and relevance to my target audience.

As previously mentioned, the cost of living was the single biggest issue that struck a note with everyone across all demographics. The idea that no government should expect people to hold down a job, work hard to pay their mortgage, rent, bills, and taxes, only for their money to be given away to people who don't, was something about which the vast majority of constituents were almost unanimous, irrespective of their political views. There was appetite across the board for Reform's agenda of tax cuts, curbing immigration, leaving the ECHR, and our views on 'woke' ideology. I got a strong sense from many undecided voters that these issues would heavily influence their decisions.

Net zero was an issue that very few thought achievable or bought into, so Reform's policy to scrap the enormous costs associated with it and all the related subsidies struck a chord with almost everybody I engaged with. People were extremely cynical about the proposals made by Labour's Shadow Secretary of State for Climate Change and Net Zero, "Red" Ed Miliband[36] who had by now morphed into a 'Green fingered' Ed Silliband. The concept of stopping the

---

[36] *Ed Milliband is a former leader of the Labour party who was caught on camera struggling with the simple task of eating a bacon sandwich in 2014.The photographs went viral at the time and were used as the perfect example of someone who couldn't handle simple tasks, didn't inspire confidence and had bitten off more than he could chew in his (unsuccessful) attempts to lead his party to an election victory the following year*

country from drilling for oil and gas, forcing us to buy it in from other countries at three times the price and at the cost of thousands of jobs, was viewed as nonsensical and delusional. On top of that was the hypocrisy of overseas travel, which has long been in the sights of net-zero politicians. They claim it's a necessity for government officials and celebrities to fly in private jets to environmental conferences all over the world, whereas a budget family holiday to less exotic locations is viewed as a luxury that should be discouraged through ever–higher and more punitive taxes.

Wednesday 26th June

Front pages:

Daily Express: FARAGE: UK MUST END FUNDING FRANCE UNTIL SMALL BOATS HALTED

Daily Mirror: LABOUR PLEDGE ON DOCS. WE'LL END 8AM SCRAMBLE

i: Public disgust at betting farce – as Tories hunt insider who leaked July election date

The Times: Labour man suspended for betting on election

Daily Mail: Starmer: Mail readers were RIGHT about Labour in 2019

The Guardian: Fifth Tory faces investigation as election betting scandal grows

The Daily Telegraph: Cabinet minister claimed he won £2k on election bet

Financial Times: Labour dragged into betting scandal after candidate backs himself to lose

There seemed to be a massive shift towards Reform, with some media reports now predicting 18 seats, which I felt sure were wildly optimistic. But, irrespective of its accuracy, it was great for morale and boosted the motivation of all of us on the campaign trail.

By now, I was so sick of the sight of my own leaflets (and indeed the image of my face that jumped from each of them..!) that I started taking more interest in those of other candidates, which had been dropped by others in the street. I'd still managed to deliver enormous numbers of them myself and made sure that I spoke to as many householders as possible on their doorsteps, depending on the time of day. As already noted, electoral rules forbid paying anyone else to do this, which would have constituted an unfair advantage, so it was down to the help of my cheerful band of volunteers, who delivered the bulk of them on my behalf. Every one of them took a minimum of a couple of hundred, some as many as five hundred, but a handful stood out. Over the course of many days, they delivered as many as five thousand of them, which was amazing, as I knew how time-consuming and incredibly hard it was.

Whilst the foot soldiers tirelessly distributed these for me without reward or complaint I also had meetings with local businesses that I had been put in contact with before returning to my favourite haunt of the various supermarkets that proliferated in the constituency. These continued to be an effective use of time. I lost count of the number of, mainly out-of-town, supermarkets that I visited, but I'm fairly sure I never visited the same one twice. I didn't set up a stall outside the stores, as I wasn't sure that the respective store managers would have approved or welcomed that, but what I was doing was no worse than "chuggers" (charity workers) shaking their collecting tins. After all, I wasn't asking people for their money, just to accept a leaflet and to consider putting their X in the box next to my name come the day.

After a long and full day of exhaustive (and exhausting) leafleting in the constituency, which had started in Kettering at 7:30 am, I'd only had some crisps for lunch. However, in the spirit of "all hands to the deck," I went to support another one of my 'Northants' colleagues, Ben Habib, at the Hind Hotel in Wellingborough, where he was the PC. Having got hopelessly lost in the one-way system there, I covered too many miles getting to know the town almost as well as I did Kettering, but could have done without the unnecessary diversion, which continued until I stumbled across a nearby car park outside what was becoming my natural habitat of yet another supermarket. I changed into smarter clothes in the back of my car.

Ben had brought along the delightful Baroness Hoey, who was better known as Kate Hoey, a Northern Ireland politician and former Labour MP for 20 years. She was there as a guest speaker to address an audience of about 40 supporters, and it was clear that the purpose of my presence was just to make up the numbers rather than engage with any of them.

Ben Habib was the party's co-deputy leader throughout the campaign and, lending another lie to the accusations of the party being racist, he was of Pakistani descent and a great ambassador as deputy leader. A successful businessman and founder of a commercial property fund, and within the confines of the allowable expenses of £20,000, he was able to throw money at his campaign trail at will. He took out advertising in local papers, printed tens of thousands more leaflets than any of the rest of us in Northamptonshire, and in the same way as US presidential candidates do, he even distributed merchandise such as paper flags and baseball caps with "Vote Ben Habib" printed on them. I thought the latter was incongruous and rather tasteless, but the country had long since adopted these

American fashion accessories to the point that they were now accepted by our fashion culture and were certainly another way of getting his name across. He also had a full-time and highly efficient campaign manager who coordinated his diary of events and appearances.

He had previously served as an MEP, which gave him the experience of a natural orator and lent him enormous credibility. He was the consummate professional in every way, he had a well-rehearsed and practiced dialogue, but his genuine sincerity and strong belief gave the impression that he genuinely had the voters' best interests at heart.

Every time I saw him in person, online, or on one of his several television appearances, I was impressed and convinced that he was an MP in waiting and was certain to occupy one of the seats that Reform was slated to win. He came across as so much better in every way than a huge number of incumbent MPs who'd been in the job for many years.

Ben was the consummate professional and totally dedicated to his own campaign and so self-centred that he didn't show any glimmer of interest in meeting me when I introduced myself to him at the bar or later. Nor was there any recognition that I had responded to his campaign manager's exhortation for support and repeated calls for troops to rally around her charge. He was completely oblivious to the fact that another PC was taking precious time out of his own campaign schedule to support a fellow candidate, to the point that on the three separate occasions I did so, he barely acknowledged my presence.

I can't say that it upset my ego, and far from being offended, I was actually very impressed by his single-minded focus. I shared his conviction that he was a top dog, and a very real prospect for being elected. I had great respect for the way he went about things and, in reality, got more out of making an appearance than not doing so, as I recognised he was a slick operator from whom I was able to learn by osmosis. In fact, it proved to be the only form of (albeit informal) guidance I was to receive from the party throughout my campaign.

Although it is now almost the norm, and maybe I'm too old-fashioned, but I could never understand how men could wear a suit without a tie. Like Nigel, Ben was always immaculately dressed in both, I did feel that the effect was rather spoilt by his habit of wearing white gym shoes. When I was at school, these were actually referred to as plimsolls, but they are now widely known as trainers for some reason. And whilst they were almost certainly examples of an expensive designer brand, to my mind, they were out of keeping with the rest of the ensemble.

As things turned out, we would share two things in common: firstly, that come the 4th of July, we would both be beaten into third place in our respective constituencies, and secondly, that, for different reasons, we both declined to attend the party conference in September.

When I returned to the supermarket to source a less-than-fresh and watery baguette for supper, which I ate in the car on the way home, I discovered that I'd exceeded their free two-hour limit in what was now a completely deserted car park and had received a parking ticket, which slightly spoilt what had been a productive and satisfying day. So much for being a loyalty card holder! I spent the journey home wondering if I should ask Sean to include this on my expenses…

***

Russell George became the fifth Tory party figure to face investigation by the gambling watchdog for allegedly placing a suspicious bet on the date of the election, as the scandal grew.

In an interview with *The New Statesman*, NF called himself the "Billy Graham" of politics and stressed his belief that his right-wing English populism could destroy the Conservatives. He also claimed that he'd "done more than anyone else to defeat the far right in Britain."

He repeated his demands that the BBC include him in this evening's TV debate with Sunak and Starmer, on the basis that Reform is now ahead of the Conservatives in the polls.

Home Office statistics were released, showing that more than 50,000 migrants had crossed the Channel since Sunak became PM. Although, of course, these figures paled into insignificance in the context of the huge net immigration figure.

Thursday 27th June

Front pages:

The Daily Telegraph: Sunak's plea to voters: Don't surrender Britain to Labour

Daily Express: NO IDEA! 9 TIMES STARMER FAILS TO GIVE AN ANSWER ON BOATS CRISIS

The Guardian: PM and Starmer clash over betting scandal in tetchy final TV debate

The Times: Sunak rams home tax message in final debate

Daily Mail: Rishi's furious blast at Starmer… YOU ARE TAKING PEOPLE FOR FOOLS!

The Independent: Starmer squares up to striking doctors: I won't give 35% rise

The scourge of social media struck again. I received proposals from people offering to boost my social media output and 're-tweet' messages for me if I set up an X account. These were usually prefaced by assurances that they would be voting for me, and I'd like to think they were all kind and genuinely meant. However, for a Luddite like me, who wasn't up to speed on 'tweeting', this was way beyond me and above my pay grade. Even if I'd had one of these accounts, it was impossible to be sure that these offers were genuine and not from troublemaking saboteurs. While I'd been able to meet my 'leafleteers' in person and make a judgment on their honesty, I couldn't do so with those offering online expertise, and I couldn't afford to risk my efforts being disrupted.

Sean passed on a warning that we all had a legal obligation to put an imprint (the party identification) on our social media, as the Electoral Commission had been complaining that not all candidates had done so. This was something that had apparently been spelled out in the "Social Media Training" session that I hadn't been offered or had the benefit of attending. After an unnecessary panic, I made sure that my Facebook page complied.

He also told us that leaving leaflets under the wipers on car windscreens was a tactic that was frowned upon and could result in complaints from the police. The British summer ensured a very high probability of rain, which would have rendered these flimsy pieces of low-grade paper into useless pulp and would have been even more annoying to recipients than having them poked through their front doors. So, I duly passed on the reminder to my merry band of helpers. I also warned them not to take shortcuts across people's gardens, even if there wasn't a dividing fence. I'd already been caught out myself by walking over a 3-foot strip of lawn and reprimanded by one angry householder who, I realised too late, already had a bright red 'Vote Labour' banner in his window although with his shaven head, string vest, and filthy, baggy tracksuit bottoms, he better fitted the image of the BNP stereotype. I suspect that, had I been a delivery driver rushing to deliver fast junk food for the already over nourished occupant, his appetite would have been such that he wouldn't have raised the issue. But it was an oversight on my part; and I should have respected that it was his patch of grass and I knew that my own time constraints were not an excuse! However, his ire was also representative of the low esteem in which politicians are generally held in this country, and I couldn't blame him for that.

As I set off for the constituency once again, I was mindful that the clock was ticking, and it was now only seven days to go until the polling stations opened. I recalled that former

Labour PM Harold Wilson had once said, "A week is a long time in politics," but I seriously wished I had rather longer than that.

I had very little sympathy with apathetic voters, as I feel that voting should be compulsory, as it is in countries like Australia. It would be easy enough to 'fine' a taxpayer or deduct payments from recipients of welfare for those who didn't vote, and it would focus the minds of those people who weren't already engaged. I found this cohort of (non) voters the most difficult to reason with, and I found they were divided into several different categories: those who felt that two-party politics and the FPTP[37] system were a sham and who would vote with their feet by not voting at all.

Secondly, there were those who simply couldn't be bothered and thought that their vote wouldn't make any difference because neither of the two main parties was sufficiently differentiated. After all, under the Conservatives, they'd already suffered from sky-high taxes, more crime, mass immigration, and poor public services. They felt that it would be the same under Labour, but the increments would just be worse and faster. Another group consisted of youngsters who were not engaged because they weren't in

---

[37] *FPTP is an acronym for the much debated and controversial First Past the Post System*

employment, so weren't paying any tax, and seemed comfortable living on our woefully generous benefits system. They didn't want to endanger their payments. They were proof that working often didn't pay, as they were disincentivised to find employment, as our punitive taxes ensured that they were better off sitting at home doing nothing.

Whichever camp they fell into, the fact was that the non-voters in this election would represent over 40% of the total electorate, dwarfing the Labour vote. The national turnout dropped to an historic low of 59.9%, the lowest since 2000. The statistics made sombre reading and were a lesson that all parties need to address in future by somehow making politics more relevant and interesting, especially to the younger generation. The key to that demographic is to do what I failed to and embrace social media.

After another day engaging with voters (and the non-voters mentioned above) in the constituency, I attended an event that evening where I was confronted by an aggressive and belligerent woman who disagreed with my contention that the NHS model was broken. It is overburdened, under-resourced, but, most importantly, badly managed by dysfunctional departmental teams who don't communicate amongst themselves, let alone with hospital trusts. Amongst its failings, there were very few benefits to be had from economies of scale when it came to processes that could be shared amongst them, especially when it came to common-sense business practices like procurement.

This lady protested at the top of her raucous voice that I was ignorant, and her simplistic view was that there was absolutely nothing wrong with this once-great institution, and that all of its issues were entirely a result of the high levels of obesity prevalent in this country. She was certainly right to say that there are far too many people who are both overweight and lazy, who could eat healthier foods and exercise more but although the WHO states that obesity does cost the NHS £6.5 billion each year, there is rather more to it than that. Hugh Bethell (author of *Get Off the Couch Before It's Too Late*) writes, "the older the already ageing society gets, the more inactive it becomes despite having more time available to take up the numerous opportunities available to take more exercise and the government and medical profession should promote the myriad ways of increasing physical activity which would certainly help relieve some of the burden on the beloved but nonetheless inefficiently run institution".

Once the increasingly verbose woman had discovered my personal interest in "environmentally unfriendly" – obviously non-electric (essentially dangerously flammable batteries on wheels, controlled by an iPad) motor cars, I was doomed in her eyes. She considered me to be someone who was obviously single handedly going out of my way to destroy the planet and her remarks got ever more personal, to the point that she insisted I was clearly over-dependent on my car and unless I wasn't careful, I would become obese myself, etc., etc. I chose not to point out that although I'm 6 ft tall, I was also roughly half her bulk, so I felt that would be unlikely. But I did point out that it was at least a 50-minute car journey back home to my corner of the county, and that it would be neither practical nor safe to try walking the 25 miles, especially as I'd be making the return journey to the constituency at the crack of dawn. The more she fed her own, more obvious dependence on alcohol, the more she refused to listen or make any rational sense and was having none of it. I found it interesting to assess how people were leaning politically and I assumed that she'd either be voting Green or Lib Dem although her demeanour was such that she might have found a more sympathetic home with the Monster Raving Loony Party. On the basis of our conversation, I didn't expect her to vote for Reform, so before her husband loaded his larger than life spouse into their even larger 'dirty' diesel fume spewing SUV to drive her home, we went our separate ways with me agreeing to disagree with her, although she resolutely refused to return the compliment. Despite the provocation, I avoided being drawn into a trap, and although tired and sorely tempted, I managed to resist the temptation to retaliate by saying that she might benefit from shedding a few pounds of weight herself and perhaps consider eating fewer doughnuts, drinking a little less alcohol and maybe even walking the few hundred yards back home rather than being driven there by her long suffering spouse.

***

An intentionally very damaging report to bring Reform into disrepute was broadcast on Channel 4 News, claiming that an undercover journalist had secretly recorded homophobic and racist comments apparently made by Reform UK canvassers while they campaigned in Clacton on behalf of Farage. One man appeared to make homophobic comments, describing a Pride flag on a police car as a "degenerate flag," and another made Islamophobia and racist slurs. Andrew Parker was heard describing Islam as "the most disgusting cult out" and suggested that army recruits should carry out “target practice” by shooting at small boats bringing illegal migrants to the UK. He also used a racial slur to refer to Prime Minister Rishi Sunak, who is of Indian descent.

Nigel made it very clear that he was "dismayed" to learn that some of his campaign team in Clacton had made reprehensible comments and that they would be taken off the team. He stated, "The appalling sentiments expressed by some in these exchanges bear no relation to my own views."

Separately, the party withdrew support from Raymond Saint, its candidate in Basingstoke, after *The Guardian* told them that he had previously been a member of the BNP. An apparent admission that the party had breached the local electoral campaign spending limit in the seat was claimed to have been a pointless and unhelpful joke by Rob Bates, who clarified the issue by pointing out that he wasn't responsible for campaign spending anyway.

Happier news for the party was an announcement that we had secured the backing of Sir John Hall, the former owner of Newcastle United FC, who had previously donated hundreds of thousands of pounds to the Conservatives but had now made a "substantial donation" to Reform.

Junior doctors began their five-day strike over pay.

Starmer criticised Sunak for a Tory party advert which showed a family with their hands in the air, with the caption: "Don't surrender your family's future to Labour."

The voting scandal continued as *The Guardian* reported that Sunak cited a 'confidential' inquiry and again refused to say whether he had told Craig Williams in advance about the election date, saying that it wouldn't be right for him to talk about it while inquiries were ongoing. Earlier, the

Metropolitan Police said seven officers were being investigated over alleged bets made on the election.

Friday 28th June

Front pages

Daily Express: BBC PAID AUDIENCE TO APPEAR AT LEADERS' DEBATE

Daily Mirror: INSIDE CRUMBLING HOSPITAL. THIS IS WHY WE NEED TO VOTE LABOUR

Daily Mail: POLL THAT SHOWS IT'S NOT TOO LATE TO STOP STARMER SUPERMAJORITY

The Guardian: Labour pledge to ban managers who silence NHS whistleblowers

The Times: Shoot illegal migrants, said Reform campaigner

i: Private school fees VAT in Reeves' first Budget but delayed until 2025

Electoral rules forbid canvassing on polling day, which meant that the Reform candidates had less than a week to go, so it was time for us all to get our heads down while our rivals made their last push to hold on to seats or cement their wins.

At the end of a week when standards, corruption, scandals, and sleaze had dominated the news ahead of key issues like the economy and immigration, the backlash over the inflammatory remarks highlighted in the Channel 4 report did us no favours at all. We all knew that it would be repeatedly aired to reinforce the misperception that the party is racist. We were conscious that there would be no undercover work on the other parties, and this ensured that in the week before the polls closed, we were now in the news-but for all the wrong reasons. At this stage, we assumed that the pair of clowns were rogue canvassers, but it was a reminder of how much trust candidates necessarily place in them when enlisting our helpers, any one of whom could have been frauds. In my case, I had done my due diligence and remained confident in my hastily assembled 'team' of volunteers.

Although a lot of damage had already been done, it wasn't long before questions arose about the dubious credentials of Andrew Parker, and rumours circulated that he was a part-time actor paid to have been a plant. If so, I assumed that this was a case of election interference, and I was relieved to hear that Essex Police were looking to establish if there had been any criminal offences in the footage. Channel 4 went on record to deny that they'd paid Parker and said: "We met Mr Parker for the first time at Reform UK party headquarters, where he was a Reform party canvasser." Despite this denial, and in light of what looked to have been a serious hit job by Channel 4, Gawain Towler from party HQ wisely took the precaution of requesting that, in order to avoid any of us being made the fall guy, we should all avoid any further interviews with their broadcasting teams across the country.

One of the emails that got my attention early that morning came from an erudite-sounding fellow called James, who emailed me (and I assume all the other respective Kettering candidates too) with a photograph of all the junk mail he'd received through his letterbox. It showed a collection of leaflets from all the respective candidates, and he berated us all for sullying his doormat in doing so, while also complaining that none of us had actually bothered to knock on his door. He was obviously either bored with too much time on his hands to have looked up all the email addresses for the respective candidates, or sufficiently interested in politics to have taken the time to do so. I had some sympathy for his plight, but for the fact that his photo did not actually show one of my Reform leaflets which was conspicuous by its absence!

I replied to him, and while I didn't have a PDF version of the offending article, I was able to send him a more environmentally friendly electronic version of the press release about me so at least he knew that a Reform candidate existed and who I was, in the unlikely event that he chose to vote for us-or indeed anyone else. Over breakfast, as I was mapping out my schedule for the day, I realised that I would be close enough to his address to make a detour, which enabled me to drop by and knock on his front door. This was easier said than done, as the postcode did not take me directly to his street, let alone his front door, which was at the end of a cul-de-sac where two of the neighbouring houses had dismantled and burnt-out cars outside them. I understood why my rivals wouldn't have been able to find it, even if they'd made the effort to try.

By the time I had knocked on his door, it was approaching midday, and it was the barking of a large dog that had clearly woken up this most unattractive character from his slumbers. It was difficult to tell from his appearance whether he was wearing his pyjamas or a tracksuit, but maybe the outfit doubled up as both, although if it was the latter, it didn't look as though it had been outside, let alone anywhere near a gym, for a very long time. Either way, it was obvious that he'd just got out of bed, so the thought occurred that he might have been a night shift worker. But if that were so, then surely he wouldn't have been emailing me in the middle of the previous night?! Whatever the case, his demeanour and questionable personal hygiene suggested that he was more likely to be someone who existed on benefits. They say that dogs often look like, and even share the characteristics of, their owners, and vice versa. While the large and salivating dog that appeared at his side when he finally opened the door was not an attractive specimen, its aggressive owner was infinitely less so.

Having introduced myself, I was subjected to a tirade of now rather less than eloquent abuse (appearances can be deceptive!) for adding to his spam by daring to respond to his email in the way that I had done, and he told me in no uncertain terms that he'd already responded to me by email. I left his doorstep relieved that I'd never have to return there- or hopefully ever meet him again. My efforts to appease a floating voter had taken a disproportionate amount of precious time to no avail, but this was part of the job, and at least I'd tried.

When I got home later that evening, I went straight into the Reform Kettering email account on my laptop and began wading through the relentless stream of correspondence addressed to me. I'd sifted out (aka deleted) the usual and tediously repetitive streams from lobbying groups and settled down to answer important ones from individuals who had real concerns about everything-from the housing shortage, schooling, the appalling condition of the roads, high levels of crime, and the state and capacity of Kettering General Hospital. In amongst them, to my great surprise, was one from James apologising for his behaviour and acknowledging the trouble I'd gone to earlier in the day! Despite this, I was pretty sure that he wouldn't have flattered me by giving me his vote, but even so, his response was somehow both satisfying and gratifying, and made the superfluous effort I had made seem more worthwhile.

Ben's assistant made a last-minute effort to rally troops by imploring all the Northants PCs to join him on the garishly liveried turquoise-coloured bus they'd secured the services of this evening. It was a shame that once again I was given so little notice of this and wasn't able to attend. If I had been able to, we might have been able to divert to my own constituency and at least drive through Kettering town centre. It was the only one of the party's few resources that was indirectly made available to me, and although I have no idea how much influence it would have had on my votes, the presence of the impressive Reform UK open-top 'battle bus' with me waving to the crowds would have provided some photo opportunities and wouldn't have done any harm. I was sorry to miss the opportunity to join Ben, but it did save me the effort of either borrowing one of his ridiculous and ill-fitting baseball hats or having to slather factor 30 something sun cream on my balding head. However, like the rest of us, I had my own campaign schedules to concentrate on, so the diminutive Ben would have been quite a lonely figure up there on his own.

***

The main news stories were dominated by last night's awful showing from US President Joe Biden in his debate with Donald Trump. However, the main UK political story continued to be the racial slurs used by a Reform canvasser against the PM's family.

Rishi Sunak said that the racist remarks made by the so-called Reform 'supporter' Andrew Parker, in the Channel 4 broadcast, calling him "an effing P***" were hurtful and unsurprisingly made him angry. He said his two young daughters "have to see and hear Reform people who campaigned for Nigel Farage" using racist language against him, and that the party leader had "some questions to answer".

Nigel repeated his assertion that the Channel 4 expose was part of an elaborate and deliberate stitch-up to smear the party and that the canvasser was an actor, saying this was "a political setup of astonishing proportions." He also stated, "This was designed to hurt us, and sadly some people believe it." Whatever the truth was, it couldn't and wouldn't be proven one way or the other until after the polls had closed and the election was over. With the rest of the predominantly left-wing media seizing on it, the tactic had, to an extent, worked. With the traction it gained on social media, a lot of damage had been achieved by the perpetrators.

Nigel also faced angry questions from a BBC *Question Time* audience over the broadcast and described the comments as a "tirade of invective abuse," but again suggested the man may have been paid. Challenged on other comments made by Reform UK candidates, Farage said he "wouldn't want anything" to do with them and claimed he had withdrawn his support.

Someone called Adrian Ramsay, who was apparently the Green Party co-leader, appeared on the same programme. Like many others, I'd never heard of him, although several of my kindly supporters suggested that I had probably achieved a higher political profile (which admittedly wasn't saying much) in the last twenty days than he had managed to over the previous twenty years! However, even he found it easy to capitalise on the uncomfortable position that Reform found itself in, as he condemned Parker's comments as "horrific," suggesting that it was "a stark reminder of the future we could be heading for if people back Reform at the election."

Nigel retorted that he had done more to drive out the far-right than any living person in British politics. He also repeated his claim that Reform offered the best opposition to Labour.

An opinion poll carried out between 24-26th June for the *i* newspaper showed that support for Reform had now fallen back from a record high of 19% the previous week to 16% after NF said the West had provoked Putin's invasion of Ukraine. The Conservatives were on 20%, up from 19% previously, but the overall picture for Sunak remained extremely bleak and left little doubt that the Conservatives were fighting a losing battle to avoid a near wipeout next week.

Saturday 29th June

Front pages:

The Guardian: Nigel Farage to boycott BBC over "biased Question Time Audience"

Daily Express: RISHI: MY HURT AND ANGER AT DAUGHTERS HEARING RACIST SLUR

The Times: Badenoch: Voters must see through Farage's act

The Independent: PM 'hurt and angry' at P-word race slur by Farage activist

Daily Mail: BORIS: BRITAIN CAN STILL SWERVE STARMERGEDDON

Juliet is my girlfriend, but as we are both in our sixties and thus classified as 'senior citizens', I struggle with the term 'girlfriend', which slightly grates as it has always struck me as more appropriate for 'twenty-something' year-olds, still in the relative flush of youth. Having debated alternatives, we could find no better description. We were definitely not 'partners', which I always think of in terms of either a business relationship or a label used by gay friends, which might have been misconstrued and confused people. Neither would she allow me to use the (admittedly one-sided) moniker of 'my admirer', so 'girlfriend' it had to be.

Anyway, this was the day she had her first experience of Kettering itself, which I was now so familiar with, as she came leafleting with me. It is amazing what a difference it made having someone else to share the burden of it all. Not only did twice the manpower (or people power in this PC world in which we live) make all the difference, but it was much less tedious having someone else to help keep your spirits up, and in this capacity she was definitely my very much-valued 'partner'!

As someone who doesn't particularly enjoy the limelight, it was odd that Juliet had previously made the rather grumpy observation at one point that I was only doing this for egotistical reasons. In fairness, this was an overreaction to the amount of time that was taken up by and I inevitably devoted to my campaign. This was despite the fact that, like my family and the vast majority of friends who were aware of it, she was hugely supportive of my efforts in standing up for what I passionately believed in and trying to shake up and reform the political landscape. It's true that certain politicians do possess overextended egos, which can grow in line with an increased profile, but the vast majority of them, of whichever political hue, do not commit themselves to the intensely hard work required. Nor do they sell their souls and sacrifice their personal lives for the amount of money they receive for doing so. Unless you're in your twenties, as so many of the inexperienced first-time Labour MPs would be, it is not massively well remunerated. For most, it is vocational and not a career to pursue if you want to make money, and as noted before, we have too many politicians but they are underpaid.

In any case, there are also much easier ways of feeding an ego, and the amount of negative and often personal comments I received-primarily from those on social media, rather than those brave enough to face up to me in person-would have shattered even the biggest ego. After a hard day's graft pounding the streets of Kettering with me, she graciously retracted her previous comments and changed her opinion on why I was doing this. However, she remained one of my greatest supporters, and her confidence in me was far greater than my own. She had even succumbed to the feedback from conversations she'd been part of or witnessed, which made her feel I had a very real chance of being elected. This made her consider the life-changing effect it would have on our lives had I been elected. However much I tried to reassure her that that was highly unlikely, she remained resolutely loyal and hopeful for me.

***

In a social media post on X, Farage said that he'd boycott the BBC, describing them as having "behaved like a political actor throughout this election". He said he would be "refusing until the BBC apologises for their dishonest *Question Time* audience" (from the previous evening) and that "Reform will be campaigning vigorously to abolish the licence fee."

NF also disowned three candidates while on the show, after being presented with their reportedly offensive remarks, saying he wanted "nothing to do with them." By necessity, all three would still appear on the ballot paper as Reform candidates, as it was too late for them to be removed. A spokesman said if any of them were elected, they would have to sit as independent MPs but that people should still vote for them if they wished to register support for Reform. NF pointed out that, "I'm not saying the situation is ideal, but the size of the Reform vote share nationally is what matters."

Reform also complained to the Electoral Commission and Essex Police about Channel 4's undercover investigation of the party and suggested that the activist who made the slur may have been a paid actor. The party reported them to the electoral watchdog, claiming they had interfered in the election. The party's secretary and leading barrister, Adam Richardson, said he would be demanding an Ofcom investigation, claiming it was "entirely evident that Mr Parker was a plant," adding that "the broadcast has clearly been made to harm Reform UK during an election period and this cannot be described as anything short of election interference." "It is wholly unbelievable that, by complete coincidence, Channel 4 was performing an undercover investigation and, by chance, were paired up to go canvassing with a man who was pretending to be someone else, using a false voice and saying almost exclusively racist and bigoted remarks. It is entirely untrue that Parker had any connection with Farage as he details in the documentary and has obviously attempted to use this fictional association to smear him in the national media and damage his campaign."

Starmer jumped on the bandwagon by saying that he shared Rishi Sunak's disgust over the remarks made and accused Farage of not doing enough after the incident, adding that it is the leader who sets the "tone, the culture, and the standards" of a political party.

Elsewhere, a speech being delivered by Farage at an election rally was interrupted when a banner mocking his views on Putin was lowered from the ceiling with a photo of the Russian president captioned "I ♥ Nigel". The campaign group with the suitably ambiguous name 'Led by Donkeys' lived up to their name and reputation by admitting responsibility for the stunt, which they said was in response to NF blaming the West for the war in Ukraine, even though what he'd actually done was predict it.

Sunday 30th June

Front pages:

The Sunday Times: Labour eyes up green belt for building blitz

The Sunday Telegraph: Labour will bankrupt every generation, warns Sunak

Daily Mirror: BE ON THE RIGHT SIDE OF HISTORY THIS TIME. VOTE LABOUR

Sunday Express: STARMER TO WRECK BRITAIN IN 100 DAYS

The Observer: Starmer's promise to voters: I will relight the fire of optimism

The Mail: RISHI WARNING: STARMER WILL WRECK BRITAIN IN JUST 100 DAYS

Another example of the party's disjointed and uncoordinated communications occurred when I learned, with only two days' notice that a pre-election rally had been planned by the party and was to be held at the NEC today. The news came from a constituent, no less! It wasn't something that had been well publicised, and the event had not been promoted or circulated to seemingly unimportant people like me. From a candidate's perspective, it seemed an odd time to hold it-only a few days before the general election, and at a time when we would all expect to be out campaigning. But maybe that's why I hadn't been told about it! It was another 'retail opportunity' for the party membership, but in fairness, the admission price was only a fiver, including parking, so I assume it was designed to cater for the party faithful and voters, rather than candidates like me, who I assume would have been expected to pay rather more for the privilege. In any case, with only four days to go until Election Day, I was far too busy to spend the whole day in attendance, not to mention the travel to and from Birmingham which is not my favourite place anyway.

Before heading off in my four-wheeled friend down the A43 once again to you-know-where, I spent the first part of the morning answering emails. The access to the Reform email address was proving to be a double-edged sword, as I was now inundated with a backlog of correspondence each day. I had to sift through and weed out the monotonous and repetitive communications. As previously mentioned, the worst of these were from lobby groups, and the frequency and volume had increased on a daily basis as we neared Election Day. They wanted to know my view on a variety of global, national, and domestic issues, ranging from defence expenditure, Palestine, and Ukraine, to abortion, the environment, and all the old chestnuts like the right to die, etc. My understanding was that these would have been sent across the board to all party candidates, and would imply that the candidate might not get their vote if they didn't agree with the respective response. Although unlikely, it was possible that we they could have all received the same response, in which case our answers would have been of no value, so I ignored them. However, there were hundreds of others from real individuals, with a host of genuine and specific concerns, apart from the cost of living and the economy-ranging from community issues like the state of Kettering General Hospital to donkey sanctuaries, to name but a few. I spent hours each evening, burning the midnight oil, answering them to the best of my abilities. Most appeared to be satisfied with my reply, but there were many who wanted an ongoing dialogue, so I tried to articulate my response in such a way that I avoided lengthy and time-consuming conversations, in the same way that I tried not to spend too much time with any one individual at their front door. This form of time management was important, but not an art I ever fully mastered, and I often found myself being invited in for a conversation and/or very welcome cups of tea.

I found that some of those who invited me into their homes also wanted to share at least part of their lives with me, by articulating their particular concerns, which meant putting them in the context of their own personal situation. I felt that the quasi-agony aunt role was a humbling experience, as people were prepared to bare their souls and put their trust in someone they had only just met. On some occasions, I would not only be introduced to other family members but more often than not, their pets too-although at least none of them could talk and take up more of my limited time. While talking to people face-to-face was genuinely interesting and one of the most rewarding and enjoyable parts of my campaign, I always had to keep moving on to somewhere else, whilst trying not to come across as rude.

After another few hours in the constituency, Juliet and I went to a drinks party local to me, where I bumped into a friend, Amy Crawfurd, the wife of a retired surgeon who had patched me up after an accident I had when a building collapsed on me several years previously in London. Amy is a very well-respected local JP, and when the subject of politics and the forthcoming election inevitably came up, she told me that in her current capacity as High Sheriff of Northamptonshire, she would be present on election night in Kettering to make the declarations as the returning officer. This came as a pleasant and welcome surprise, although I was too embarrassed to admit that I hadn't realised she'd reached such exalted heights of public office.

We were warned about allegations that candidates had been offered incentives to stand down and were asked to let the party know as soon as possible about any approaches we might receive from Conservative candidates or their teams. I was disappointed that no one thought it was worth bothering to 'reach out' to me, and of course, had they done so, I would have rejected the offer of any financial bribes. But there's a price for everything, and I would have been curious to know how much any cowboys thought I was worth, and what 'price' they might have put on the head of this particular "Indian"!

***

The end of a difficult week for Reform, in which they had to suspend three candidates after offensive remarks and face the fallout from Channel 4's questionable smears, culminated in the announcement of a last-minute defection by Liam Booth-Isherwood. He claimed there was a "significant moral issue" in parts of the party, following what he called “reports of widespread racism and sexism.” In announcing he was dropping out of the race, he said he would instead be endorsing Tory contender Maggie Throup in the seat of Erewash in Derbyshire.

Richard Tice retaliated by repeating what we had earlier been warned about: candidates being offered jobs and inducements “to persuade them to talk badly of Reform, stand down, and then endorse the Tory candidate." He said there were “dark forces at play by desperate Tories.”

Future party chairman Zia Yusef, Tice, and Anne Widdecombe all addressed thousands of supporters at the ‘Rally for Reform’ at the NEC, but the star turn was Nigel Farage, who, despite all the challenges, told an enraptured audience: “I’m actually quite bullish for what happens in the next 5 days,” he said. “Do you know what? We’re going to surprise you all!”

Monday 1st July

Front pages:

The Times: Sunak turns fire on Farage in battle for the undecided voters

i: UK heading for ‘stagnation’ after election, Labour and Tories told

Daily Express: KEMI: MY HEART BREAKS WHEN TORIES TURN TO REFORM

The Guardian: Labour can stem populist threat by improving lives, says Starmer

Daily Mail: DON'T LOCK IN LABOUR FOR A GENERATION

The Tennis Championships began at Wimbledon today but came too late to create a worthwhile distraction for many traditional Conservative voters whose minds were already made up not to vote them in for another term.

There was definitely a sense of relief for me that, in motor racing terms, I had made it onto the final straight and was within sight of the finish line. Even though I didn't expect to take the chequered flag as the winner, I hoped that I had at least done a sufficiently respectable job. What's more, I hadn't (yet) fallen flat on my face, despite the hurdles that I had encountered along the way, but there was still a lot to be done. The news that Reform UK now had more than 60,000 paid-up members was extraordinary and was another sign of increasing momentum, which was enough to put a spring in my step as I headed back down the A14 to Kettering early that morning.

I empathised especially with one particular forty-something-year-old, hardworking couple who invited me into their house. I managed to convince them of the merits of the party and the need for Reform. Both of them were previously staunch Labour voters, and neither they nor any member of their respective families had ever voted for any other party. So, as it was with me, it was a very big decision for them to change the allegiance of a lifetime. Although cautious about doing so, they resolved to spread the word, at the very least to their extended family, and bravely were prepared to be pilloried for doing so. However, it was interesting that they remarked that they probably wouldn't be "telling their neighbours," and it was my loss that none of those were at home, so I didn't have the opportunity to speak to any of them and try to win their votes too. It was sad, and I felt it was wrong that attitudes were such that anybody should feel there was a stigma attached to casting your vote one way or another.

I repeated my mantra that, whilst even the eternal optimists recognised that Reform was unlikely to win the election this time, all our votes were about building the necessary momentum ahead of the next election, and in the process, becoming the main opposition party. They were reassured by my message that if we managed to secure a handful of seats, namely between three and five, the party would have gained the requisite widespread acceptance and sufficient respect that would make it much easier for people like them to be less shy and more vocal and public about their choice.

***

The Daily Telegraph posed the question as to whether Nigel Farage had stumbled at the last hurdle.

Reform UK said that the party leader had engaged the legal services of Carter-Ruck over a Mail on Sunday story quoting Volodymyr Zelensky condemning him as being "infected with the 'virus of Putin.'" In a video message posted yesterday on X, Farage said, "Ten years ago, I predicted there would be war in Ukraine because I thought Putin would use NATO and EU expansion." But he added, "I've never supported his administration in any way."

Rishi Sunak warned that Vladimir Putin wanted Labour to win the election because they would weaken the UK's security and fuel Russian aggression by failing to invest more in our defence and armed forces.

The Prime Minister also said he had 'absolutely not' given up hope of the Conservatives winning, despite talking about the prospect of a Labour "supermajority." As he was mentally preparing himself for the worst, he told the BBC his party had not "got everything right" and said he understood people's frustrations with him and the Conservatives. This would stand as one of the greatest understatements of his unsuccessful and fruitless campaign.

Tuesday 2nd July

Front pages:

The Times: Starmer: A big majority will be best for Britain

Daily Express: Voting Reform 'risks losing hundreds of Tory MPs for a generation'

The Daily Telegraph: Royal Mail blamed for postal vote chaos

i: Labour faces up to prospect of far-right neighbour in France with early talks

The Guardian: Labour would take global lead on climate

Metro: NEVER MIND THE BALLOTS

The Northamptonshire Telegraph article on me appeared online, together with another version of the photo of an apparently one-eared me alongside one of Nigel Farage, which was the nearest I got to him over the course of the campaign.

Having been on the road and on my feet since 6:30 in the morning, I was now desperate for sustenance. I bought a hot dog from a street seller. In warm and sunny weather, it wouldn't have been my first choice of food or vendor, but my day was such a frenzied rush and I really needed something to eat quickly. There were no 'Golden Arches' nor fast food outlets to be found but I reasoned that I ought to be supporting an enterprise from the local community rather than an American-owned chain. Added to which, it was bound to be cheaper. I was wrong on both counts, as it was served up by an unsmiling lady and her partner, neither of whom spoke barely a word of English. They charged me £12.00 for what was described as a 'New York hotdog' (a very short frankfurter in an even shorter bread roll) and a further £6.50 for 'cheesy chips' (a very small carton of fries with a teaspoon of grated cheese on top). It didn't constitute a 'Happy Meal' for me, but it should have been for her. So, I did feel that she could at least have done me the courtesy of offering me a smile by way of showing her appreciation and satisfaction after shamelessly 'robbing' me and making at least several hundred percent profit in the process. But maybe it was just the Reform UK rosette that she disapproved of...? It's never a great feeling to know that you've been ripped off, however I was in too much of a hurry to question her business model, although it was good to know that the spirit of entrepreneurship was alive and well in Kettering. I had to admire their spirit, but was relieved that she didn't try to surprise me further and insult my intelligence by trying to add on a so-called 10–15% 'service' charge as well.

What sometimes became a pressing issue when on the road for so long was answering the occasional call of nature, and this brought to mind another quote from Margaret Thatcher about 'pee breaks,' as the Iron Lady obviously had an iron bladder too. During the 1979 election campaign, journalist Ann Leslie asked if the Tory campaign bus could make more frequent lavatory stops as her bladder had been weakened by giving birth. Thatcher gave her a withering look. "No one needs to go more than twice a day," she said. "I go first thing in the morning and then at night, and it's quite enough."

Like Farage, I enjoy a pint or two (lager in my case) and also like ice cream. But while some of my supporters did arrange for me to meet small groups in informal meet-and-greet sessions in the odd local pub, I didn't have a driver to ferry me around, so drinking while campaigning wasn't an option for me. Neither did the idea of talking with my mouth full of ice cream appeal to me in the same way as it obviously did for our leader. Invariably, I found myself sipping a cup of tea, which seemed a bit incongruous when surrounded by enthusiastic supporters refreshing themselves on something a bit stronger.

As D-Day got closer, the levels of abuse got worse. Unlike some of my PC colleagues, I rarely experienced any on the streets of Kettering or the villages. The higher your social media profile, the more you got online, and although I did have my share of that, we all agreed that the bulk of the aggression and intolerance came from Labour supporters. While those from other parties might disagree with us, the flack tended to be much more polite and respectful.

A couple of colleagues reported that they'd seen Reform posters they'd placed torn down in places near to where houses had Labour banners in their windows, although I didn't have that problem as my requests to party HQ for posters had fallen on deaf ears. Similarly, I hadn't been able to provide any of those of my constituents who asked for them with promotional stickers for their homes or cars. In retrospect, I felt that was probably a good thing because, in areas where feelings ran particularly high, this could invite vandalism, and I didn't want to be indirectly responsible for any of my supporters having their cars keyed or even bricks thrown through windscreens or the windows of their houses, as reportedly happened in other parts of the country. When my membership card finally arrived 9 months later, it was accompanied by a pointless apology of a sticker, not much bigger than one of Nigel's fag packets, and wouldn't have made any impression on the back of an iPhone, let alone a window or a car. If it was intended to be a token of gratitude for my membership of the party, it was to prove far greater recognition than I ever received for my efforts as a Parliamentary Candidate!

***

In an irresponsibly last-minute and cynical move, Georgie David let down all her constituents and wasted their votes by becoming the second Reform UK candidate to jump ship and switch allegiance to the Conservatives, which was unforgivable. Even more disgraceful was her accusation that the vast majority of those like me standing for the party in the election were "racist, misogynistic, and bigoted," and she accused the party of failing to tackle the problems of racism and prejudice in its ranks. She had been standing for West Ham and Beckton and issued a statement through the Conservatives, whom she was now backing.

It was again Richard Tice who responded by suggesting that the Conservatives had sought to infiltrate the party with fake candidates: "Desperate toxic Tories sent us some Trojan horse candidates by offering jobs, safe council seats, etc., to spread lies," he said on X.

It was an appalling insult, and everyone in the party took her uneducated remarks very personally. Reflecting their candidates' views, the party said: "We strongly disagree with her sweeping comments about the 'vast majority' of our 600-plus candidates, most of whom she can never even have met. And we find it sad and strange that she chose not to bring up any of her concerns with the party leadership before publicly trashing so many of her blameless colleagues who are giving their all to get Reform UK elected."

Reform UK faced more pressure because of historic comments made by their candidate in the Orkney and Shetland constituency, after *The Times* alleged he'd posted numerous insults about prominent women on social media, which were said to include advocating that former First Minister of Scotland, Nicola Sturgeon, should be 'shot.'

Once again, it was down to our chairman, Richard Tice, to defend the party. He told BBC Radio 4, "Obviously appalling, absolutely appalling. But I'm very clear; we're a new political party. We've been growing fast. Of course, like anybody, we make some mistakes." The party would make it clear that it wanted 'much stricter control' over candidate selection for Reform and that 'there were some people there that should never, ever have been there.' That was also true for all parties, but the media bias against Reform meant that their 'rogues' were always the most publicised.

Keir Starmer claimed that right-wing populism was "a really serious issue" in the UK and across Europe, adding that part of the answer was to understand why people had "lost faith in politics." He was absolutely right on the latter point but was on very dangerous ground and hypocritical in the extreme to highlight 'Partygate,'[38] especially as it was later suggested that, despite being so vocal about the issue, he too had personally breached lockdown rules when opposition leader by having a 'voice coach' travel to London on Christmas Eve 2020.

Whatever the truth, any 'lessons' that he might have received while the rest of us were settling down to seasonal festivities didn't make any difference and did nothing to improve either his much-criticised drawl or his monotone style of delivery. He should have asked for a refund. A good speaker, he is not.

Wednesday 3rd July

Front pages:

The Times: Boris: Big Labour is pregnant with Horrors

The Daily Telegraph: Boris: It's not too late to stop Labour

Daily Mail: Boris and Rishi unite to stop Starmergeddon

Daily Express: Rishi: YOUR VOTE COUNTS, YOUR VOICE COUNTS...PLEASE USE IT WISELY

---

[38] Partygate was the description of a political scandal which surrounded social gatherings of government and Conservative Party staff during the COVID pandemic of 2020 and 2021, when public health restrictions prohibited most meetings.

The Guardian: Backlash over 'antiemetic' Tory attack on Starmer

Daily Mirror: 14 YEARS OF HURT NEVER STOPPED US DREAMING...

The Independent: The final poll: Tories brace for total wipeout

To no one's great surprise, except perhaps the soon-to-be-ousted PM who remained in denial until the very last possible moment, Labour was on course to win the biggest majority since 1832. Starmer had expressed concerns that his voters were so assured of victory that they might not bother to turn out at all, although the Reform candidates couldn't afford to be complacent in any way. PCs are not allowed to campaign on polling day, so this represented the last opportunity for a final push. However, there was not yet any sense of calm before the storm because my work was far from over.

It was to be another very early start for what I knew was going to be a very long day, although I had been buoyed by the promise of strong support when out and about in the last few days.

All of us on 'Team Northants' exchanged wishes of good luck with each other on the WhatsApp group for our last day of campaigning, and Sean advised that we should all try to get some rest before the big day tomorrow.

I didn't get back from Kettering until after 10:00 pm, having done over 25,000 steps that day. I rewarded my effort with an overcooked supermarket pizza and a beer before logging onto my laptop and beginning my now habitual late-night ritual of opening the constituency emails. As usual, this involved weeding out the ones from the interminable lobbyists who, all credit to them, persisted in barraging me right up until the last minute, and responding to those from people with genuine addressable concerns and questions.

Thankfully, by this stage of my necessarily abbreviated campaign, the majority of those I received on both my personal and Reform email accounts were warm and heartfelt wishes of good luck for the next day. However, I realised that the normally highly efficient Electoral Services department hadn't responded to my request from a few days earlier for a list of the locations of all the polling stations, so I began the laborious task of Googling them all before turning in for what was left of the night. This went against the strong advice that Sean had given, ahead of tomorrow, which was going to entail a very long night with only tea, coffee, sugary drinks, and basic snacks available at the venue to keep us going.

I was pretty sure he wasn't being serious, but, as my agent, Sean Lever had earlier sent instructions as to what I should say in the unlikely event that I was voted in as the local MP. I was to: thank the returning officer, thank the counting staff, and most of all, thank the people of Kettering who had put their faith in me.

It was with amusement that, before I finally went to bed, I re-read his message in which he reminded me to promise to do my best to represent the best interests of each and every one of the constituents-not only those who had put their faith in me, but also those for whom I may not have been their first choice. Also, that I'd look forward to meeting many more of them over the course of the next Parliament and working together towards common goals, etc. etc. As my head hit the pillow, I began composing my improbable speech, and got as far as "I'm overwhelmed with appreciation…" And then I was fast asleep.

***

A YouGov MRP poll this evening suggested that Keir Starmer's party could win 431 seats, leaving the Tories with just 102 MPs. The consensus was that the Tories were bracing themselves for a total wipeout, whilst Labour was on course for one of the biggest victories in history.

In a stunt that the easily forgettable Ed Davey (leader of the Lib Dems, for those of you who have already understandably forgotten) would have been proud of-and which even smacked of Vladimir Putin's macho image-Nigel Farage arrived in Clacton to rally the troops in a decommissioned ex-army vehicle. He wasn't driving it, but as it reversed through the crowds and he chanted "We want our country back," the vehicle narrowly avoided hitting one of his supporters on a mobility scooter. Had there been any contact, it would have rather spoiled the show.

Maintaining the pugilistic and defiant message, he was later seen posing in a boxing ring with two-time world heavyweight boxer Derek Chisora, sporting a pair of Reform-branded boxing gloves.

Rishi Sunak optimistically insisted that the election result was not a 'foregone conclusion,' saying, "The game isn't over until the final whistle goes," and, "There's fight in the underdog," although no one was quite sure whether he was talking about tomorrow's election or football. But, ever the pragmatist, Mel Stride was correct with his prediction when he said that it was "highly likely" that Labour would achieve the largest majority in history.

In warning against complacency, Starmer pointed out that, "Change only happens if you vote for it," which reflected real concerns that Labour voters were so assured of victory that they might not bother to turn out at all.

Meanwhile, Ed Davey, no doubt looking forward to a break from travelling to and from adventure playgrounds up and down the country, proclaimed that "There is no ceiling on Lib Dem ambitions," which was a typically ambiguous non-statement that conjured up images of him taking a ride in the London Eye, overlooking the Houses of Parliament, perhaps in order to attempt to get a fresh perspective on Westminster.

Thursday 4th July

Front pages:

The Daily Telegraph: Homeowners face council tax raid under Labour

Daily Mail: Vote Farage, get them...

Daily Mirror: Vote for change. Vote Labour

The Guardian: Starmer hails 'new age of hope' as Britain votes in historic election

The Times: Labour set for biggest majority since 1832

i: Labour's lead narrows in final poll, but Starmer still on course for landslide

Daily Express: VOTE TORY

The Independent: Tories on just 82 seats? No wonder they've given up

Financial Times: Tories braced for bleak night as polls put Labour back on track for landslide win

Metro: THE NATION DECIDES

Daily Star: Toodle pip!

The 'D' day of reckoning had finally arrived, and although I was aware that the forthcoming US Presidential debate was more consequential for British politics than anything that happened in this country, today still represented a big decision for UK voters, and I was very proud that I was able to play a small part in it.

The first message I read this morning was from Richard Tice, thanking all of us for our hard work and efforts for Reform UK, and wishing us a fantastic day, which was much appreciated. There was more swapping of pleasantries and messages of good luck between us all on WhatsApp, together with final words of encouragement from Sean, who said that we all deserved to win today!

Ahead of what was going to be a very long, challenging (26 hours) day and night, the first thing I did was walk over to my village hall to cast my own vote for my colleague Paul Hogan, who was standing in the South Northamptonshire constituency where I lived. After all the blood, sweat, and tears, I missed the satisfaction that other candidates had in voting for myself, which would have been a novel experience. But I comforted myself that Paul himself was in a similar position, as he too lived in a different constituency to the one in which he was standing.

Thankfully, as I had worked into the early hours of the night, I had cleared most of the emails, and I wasn't greeted with the unwelcome sight of too many more. I did receive the list of polling stations, which I'd requested from Electoral Services. It was irritating, as I'd stayed up extra late the previous evening putting together a route map to get to as many of them as possible in the most time-efficient way, and could have really done with the extra sleep.

Again, I had breakfast on the hoof, consisting of a fruit smoothie I'd prepared the night before and a mug of coffee, which I don't normally drink because it affects my sleep so badly. However, on this occasion, I knew I'd need it and would be very grateful if it succeeded in keeping me awake later that night. By the time I reached the first of the many polling stations I would visit over the course of the next ten hours or so, I was set up for the day and relieved that I'd managed to avoid spilling either of my drinks over my freshly ironed shirt.

Scottish First Minister John Swinney had written to Sunak calling for a review of the postal voting system, which was not only open to abuse but also unreliable. Delays in delivering postal votes meant that a great many holidaymakers did not receive their ballots before going away, but Downing Street said they were "working closely with the Electoral Commission, returning officers, Royal Mail, and the print suppliers to support the resolution of these issues." Royal Mail had denied there was any problem with ballot papers being sent out, but the dialogue on our WhatsApp group today proved otherwise. It was buzzing with reports of people all over the country who had applied for postal votes that hadn't arrived, and who were not allowed to vote at their polling station in person.

The Northants constituents were reportedly being asked to go to Kettering to get a replacement vote and then return to their polling station a second time, which was obviously easier for my constituents, but even some of them wouldn't have been able to get to the council offices without me acting as a go-between and connecting handfuls of individuals with others who were prepared to drive them.

Candidates weren't allowed into the polling stations, but whenever one of the staff members came out for a fag break or fresh air, I made a point of speaking to them. Each of them told me that the footfall was higher than usual I was approached throughout the day by scores of supporters telling me they'd voted for me. It was humbling to meet people who said that they had actually done so, rather than promising that they would, which was less reliable.

News services and media outlets were banned from publishing commentary on the day, and similarly, candidates had been warned of the strict rules that we couldn't leaflet or canvass outside polling stations. Neither were we allowed to put up posters in the immediate vicinity, but that still wasn't going to be an issue for me. Although, it wouldn't have surprised me if some were dispatched by party HQ after the election was over.

There wasn't much else I could do, but I'd been advised to get around to as many of the polling stations in my constituency as possible and stand outside them wearing my now very well-worn and bedraggled Reform rosette, a smile, and a friendly face. I was told that it's the last thing voters will see before they cast their vote, and that it would have an impact, which sounded ambiguous. Sean had said to "just look pretty," which, in my case, would be stretching the imagination a little, and I thought might be counterproductive. Although if it didn't actually put voters off, then at least those who had seen the awful photos of me could see that I did actually possess both ears, even though they were not to know that I was almost deaf in one of them.

The theory was that some sort of visibility was important, and certainly better than no presence. To that end, I expected to see my candidates from other parties doing the same, and even envisaged a level of unseemly verbal fisticuffs and sparring between some of us. But I was surprised that the only other candidate I saw throughout the day was Emily Fedorowycz from the Green Party. I chatted to her, less about politics but more about the campaign trail and the process, and her dog, which accompanied her to some of the stations. She was absolutely charming, and irrespective of our obviously differing views, she was a very credible candidate as a local MP with her background in the local community, which, although the idea conjured up an image of a garden gnome in my mind, included her being the first-ever 'green mayor.'

I was almost a little disappointed not to have seen any other candidates doing the rounds. Maybe they were resting ahead of the long night ahead, but it worked in my favour as a lot of voters talked to me before casting their votes, and it was very clear that there were many who were still undecided up until the point when they arrived at the polling station. I was surprised by the number of well-wishers who bid me "Good luck," although it was obvious that not all of them were supporters, because some delivered their message in distinctly sarcastic tones.

***

The weather in Northamptonshire was hot and sunny, so I was grateful for the temperamental sunroof and air con in my ageing but trusty steed, which had served as my own rather more discreet personal 'campaign bus' compared to the huge double-decker that the party had pressed into service.

Most of my day had consisted of driving between polling stations and then 'loitering' outside them, attempting to smile reassuringly at people, so my step count was much lower than yesterday's had been. However, I was conscious of the need for a break ahead of the long night ahead. I also had to change from shirt sleeves into a suit and tie in order to look more presentable for the count and photographs that would be taken on the stage when results were declared.

Although I hadn't managed to get around all the polling stations, I did visit sixteen of them in total and had strategically covered those in the areas where I felt I'd gained the most traction and stood a better chance of votes. But by recent standards, I left the constituency early. After the 50-minute drive, I got back home at 7.30 pm, in time to meet Juliet, who had voted (also for Reform, thankfully) in her constituency and driven up from Somerset to lend her support for the long night ahead-and, most importantly, as it turned out, to help keep me awake. I had time for a quick shower and a change into my suit before we returned to Kettering town centre.

Polling stations closed at 10.00 pm, and counting wouldn't start until the ballot boxes were delivered to the counting hall at Kettering Conference Centre, which made us quite relaxed about the time that we actually arrived at the count. The town centre was unusually quiet when we arrived, despite there being no Euro football matches on that evening. But perhaps the residents were more interested in the fourth day of the tennis championships at Wimbledon. We found a great Italian restaurant called 'Casa di Roma,' which, counter-intuitively, was owned and managed by a charming Indian couple who produced the most delicious meal for us in their almost deserted restaurant.

The proprietor saw the rosettes we were both sporting and engaged us in conversation about politics and the parlous state of the country, with a particular gripe about the effects of energy prices and business rates on his own enterprise. Born in India, he and his wife had spent 20 years in Holland before arriving here and becoming hardworking, taxpaying citizens in the UK. But they were now seriously contemplating a return to the Netherlands due to the cost of living and the difficulties that a small business such as his had endured in making ends meet. I didn't ask them who they had cast their vote for, but whether or not it was for me, we seemed to have a meeting of minds on all the major issues, including uncontrolled immigration.

There were three constituencies being counted at the venue, which meant that, together with me, two other Reform candidates, Ben Habib and Eddie McDonald, were there with their respective teams. Sean had never been to the WNC venue but had told us that, although he had seen declarations made as late as 5.00 am in the past that was only when recounts were needed. He was confident that, provided it was a straightforward count, they were likely to be made nearer to 3.00 am. He was wrong!

There was no protocol as to what to wear for the count, but I wore a suit which, unlike the one that my son had photographed me in, was a rather better fit. However, as the night turned out to be much longer than any of us expected, pyjamas might have been more appropriate, although perhaps not such a good look in the inevitable photos that would be taken throughout the evening.

The Conference Centre was home to the vast counting hall full of teams of long-suffering tellers manually checking tens of thousands of ballot papers, sorting them into piles before they were double-checked, counted, and then recounted. It was a soulless job and such a thankless task that I almost felt guilty for the part I'd played in creating it, but they executed it all with great patience and in complete silence. It was no surprise that they looked extremely bored doing their necessarily tedious jobs, and I had huge empathy for them, even though I presumed and hoped that they were being well rewarded for their night shift.

If marking an "X" on a ballot paper seemed unnecessarily antiquated, then manually counting tens of thousands of them in this day and age seemed almost prehistoric. A 5-minute circuit of the hall to witness the archaic process was worse than watching paint dry for us “spectators” and even made cricket look interesting! For those of us who didn’t enjoy either of those pastimes, it was more a test of endurance and extreme patience for all involved, even though all the candidates and supporting teams had a vested interest in making sure that the teams of tellers added the appropriate ballot papers onto the correct piles.

Sean was there by the time we arrived, and I was amused to note that he was sporting a different rosette to mine (ref photo p.158). If not actually bigger, it was certainly a more recent design than the handful he’d passed on to me at our first meeting, and I now realised that they had not only been second-hand but also from last ‘season,’ so if nothing else they fitted with my reputation for being fashionably out of date. It seemed to represent the lack of support, interest, or respect that the party had for last-minute candidates like me. However, no one else seemed to notice, and it was too late to bother me now.

Sean's enthusiasm and knowledge kept the spirits of us three candidates up, despite everyone fighting back the urge to sleep, partly because of the time of night and partly because of the all-pervading boredom. The monotony was relieved by the declarations, which were announced from all over the country on the one and only small TV screen situated in a corner of the entrance hall outside the counting hall. It was watched intently by the various party candidates and their guests. It was positioned next to the bar, which would have been convenient had it been allowed to sell alcohol on such an important occasion. Although it was probably just as well that it couldn't, as things could have got rowdy between the opposing candidates if booze had been permitted. In my case, it would almost certainly have ensured that I nodded off to sleep on even more occasions than I actually did. Juliet was constantly having to wake me up from my slumber, as it was, so black coffee was the order of the day (and night), and probably more appropriate.

Each candidate was able to invite a handful of guests to the count, and whilst I obviously had to be there for the declaration, I couldn't understand why anyone other than perhaps family members (mine all politely declined) would want to spend what turned out to be almost nine hours in the venue I invited some of my most loyal and willing helpers and expected to receive a range of politely creative excuses for non-attendance from them. However, I was surprised and pleased that several of them, including Ian Blackwell, Carole Shrigley, and Christine Manning, amongst others, not only turned up but stayed there to support me until the bitter end. I was really grateful for their enthusiasm. They'd been part of the journey and wanted to see it all the way through with me, which was very much appreciated.

A good and needlessly loyal friend of ours, Richard Frankel, was one who didn't offer any side-splittingly unfunny excuses and joined us at about one o'clock in the morning to lend some moral support and provide a much-needed break from the monotony. Like most of us present he'd never been to an election count and was interested to witness it all. Although, after twenty minutes, even his enthusiasm for the proceedings had understandably dissipated, but his humour and presence provided a much-needed tonic for Juliet and me, and we were sorry when his patience finally deserted him, and he left to go home, unable to contain his excitement or stay awake any longer.

I was pleased to finally meet the journalist Sam Wildman from the *Northamptonshire Telegraph* face-to-face, as he and the newspaper had kindly given me such welcome and helpful coverage. The result was now all in the lap of the gods, and whilst I now felt like a bit of a spare part with nothing more I could do to enhance my chances further, he was there with all his peers to report on proceedings and had a lot more to do than any of us candidates. Despite this, he still looked much perkier than I felt by the end of the night, which was probably something to do with him being about half my age.

I also made a point of engaging with several of the other candidates; after all, we were all in this together. In the same way that the German and British soldiers laid down their arms in WW1 on Christmas Day 1914 in a truce, in which they left their trenches to meet in no man's land to play football and share their provisions with their adversaries, I felt there should be a break in 'hostilities.'

Were it not for the fact that it was full of people counting ballot papers, the conference centre would have easily been big enough to accommodate a football match. But although I didn't expect that any of the candidates or their teams would be whiling away the time (and there was enough of it!) playing games with each other, there was a sense of camaraderie between most of us. I did make the effort to talk to other candidates and their supporters, who were civil, and some even genuinely friendly.

The Labour acolytes were far too self-important and protective to allow me anywhere near their charge, which was a pity as I would have liked to have met her. Retrospectively, I felt that I might even have been able to give her a few tips on how to deliver her imminent acceptance speech. However, I did reconnect with Emily and met some of her campaign team, including her father, and they even shared some of their snacks with us, which was a nice touch, proving the point that political enemies can be friends and at least have respect for each other and their opinions, even if they are at odds with their own.

I went out of my way to seek out Philip Hollobone but wish I hadn't bothered, as he displayed all the characteristics and complete lack of charm that constituents had forewarned me of when I introduced myself. I didn't expect him to welcome me with open arms but I proffered him my hand out of courtesy and by way of sportsmanship, which was returned with a muttering of unprintable profanities, followed eventually by an unpleasantly weak handshake. I gathered that he didn't subscribe to the spirit of "all's fair in love and war!" He would have been aware for a long time that he was just about to lose his job, but that wasn't just because of me. Although, had I been allowed more time by the infuriating and inefficient organisation of Reform UK, I'm very confident that I would have soundly beaten him into third place and his unpalatable behaviour made me wish even more that I had done.

To relieve the intense boredom, every hour or so, Juliet and I would leave our places by the 'dry' bar next to the one and only TV monitor and go back into the hall to see what was going on. This was partly to lend moral support to the counting staff, who were relentlessly beavering away, but also in anticipation that the declarations were close to being called. We were always disappointed to find that they weren't. I can't imagine that he would have been on tenterhooks, but each time we did a lap of the vast room, we saw Hollobone and his companion on the sidelines watching proceedings intently. The only time he lifted his eyes was to glare at us, which served only to make me walk past him time and again in a puerile attempt to irritate him. As well as providing a modicum of entertainment for me, the tactic clearly worked. His demeanour was most unpleasant, and it made Juliet feel quite uncomfortable, so I was very pleased that he lost his seat-and so comprehensively too.

One of the few moments of relative excitement was provided when one of my team thought they'd seen more crates piled high with ballot papers for the Greens than for me and Reform. But that proved to be a temporary aberration and could have been the result of hallucination due to sleep deprivation. In truth, there was not much sense of anticipation, as there was never any doubt about who would win. It was more about just how many votes the arrogant and ungracious Hollobone would lose to Labour by. Rather like Donald Trump, he had been a prime example of how voters don't need to actually like a politician in order to give them their vote.

In the event, none of us three Reform candidates being counted at the Kettering Conference Centre won our respective seats, but the newly elected Labour candidates all trotted out similarly worded, pre-prepared speeches. Although Rosie Wrighting, who won the Kettering seat, droned on interminably as though she'd just won an Oscar for Best Youngest Actress at a Hollywood awards ceremony. She read out what seemed an unnecessarily long list of thanks to those who had helped her campaign, starting with her mother and several other relatives. If it hadn't been so late (actually, by this time, early in the morning), I'm sure that several of her supporters would have got emotional and shed a few faux tears. But most of those of us still present had zoned out and were asleep on our feet, so the new MP might just as well have been thanking her pet gold fish for all any of us cared by that time.

I didn't envisage that the experience of standing on the rostrum with all the other similarly impatient and sleep deprived candidates would be quite as elating as standing on the podium after a motor race. However, the unglamorous setting of the vast and soulless conference centre was definitely not Hollywood or Monaco and by now, the one thing everybody, irrespective of their politics, had in common was that we all wanted to get out of the place and back home as quickly as we reasonably could to catch up on some well-earned rest. After a brief speech from the deservedly ousted Conservative MP (aka 'Mr Angry'), there was a rush for fresh air, daylight, and the car park.

One of the highlights of the interminable wait was bumping into our friends Amy and Edward Crawfurd. Amy, of course, was there in her official capacity as High Sheriff of Northamptonshire, and it was her duty to announce the declarations in her role as returning officer. She was looking very smart in her regalia, but when we first spotted them, she made it very clear that I shouldn't kiss her hello, presumably in case anyone thought that this might be a show of favouritism or bias, although of course, she took no part in the actual counting process, so couldn't influence it in any way, even had she wanted to. It was just our luck that Kettering was the last of the three constituencies to be declared. But once we'd left the podium, Amy-still looking as fresh as a daisy (which I definitely did not look or feel)-did come bouncing up to say, "You can kiss me now!" which I did, both as a belated hello but now more urgently also as a goodbye, as by now, we were all raring to get away as quickly as we possibly could.

***

Exit polls had initially indicated that Reform might win up to 13 seats, but true to form, they were hopelessly inaccurate and, in our case, wildly optimistic. By the morning, it was clear that the Tories had received a massive kick in the ballots and Labour had secured a landslide victory. More importantly, Reform UK had won four seats, including Farage, who became an MP for the first time in eight attempts by winning his seat in Clacton. He was joined by Richard Tice (Boston and Skegness), Rupert Lowe (Great Yarmouth), ex-Conservative MP Lee Asworth (Ashfield), and, after an incredibly close finish, they were later joined by James McMurdock (South Basildon and East Thurrock) to give Reform UK a magnificent and historic result of five seats in the House of Commons. It was an outstanding achievement.

In terms of vote share and proportional representation, the party finished in third place and had won an incredible 4,003,648 votes overall, representing 14.3% of the total vote. This was more than the Lib Dems, who received 3,366,290 votes, yet under the vagaries of the First Past the Post system, they won 68 seats.

It was very good fortune for the Conservatives, and to a lesser extent Labour, that our 4.1 million votes were spread too evenly to translate into any more seats. It was notable that Reform averaged just one seat in Parliament for every 823,000 people who voted for us, whereas the Lib Dems, with their well-established infrastructure and experience, won a seat for every 49,000 votes. The Tories won a seat for every 56,000 votes, and for Labour, winning 411 of the 650 seats, it equated to 23,600 votes per seat.

A video posted overnight by Nigel on X was entitled: "The revolt against the establishment is underway."

Friday 5th July

Front Pages

The Times: Exit Poll Puts Labour on Course for Landslide

Daily Express: CRUSHING BLOW TO TORY PARTY IN ELECTION

Independent: Landslide!

Daily Mirror: KEIR WE GO

The Daily Telegraph: Labour Landslide

Daily Mail: LABOUR SET FOR HISTORIC LANDSLIDE

i: Labour Landslide

Metro: KEIR STORMER

The Guardian: Huge Labour Majority Predicted by Exit Poll

We were drunk, sadly not on alcohol thanks to the dry bar (a contradiction if ever there was one) at the Kettering

Conference Centre, but from exhaustion. The adrenaline that our bodies had been able to muster over the course of a long and extremely unexciting, anticlimactic night had peaked and worn off completely. We were barely able to keep our eyes open. It was daylight when we left, and at an hour when most people were either still fast asleep or getting up ready to go to work for the last day of the week, our journey home was interrupted only by the illogical and inconsistent speed restrictions imposed by the various local Northamptonshire councils. I fully expected these to get even worse now that they were under Labour control.

Juliet and I got back home at just before 8:00 am and immediately fell into bed, exhausted, happy, and satisfied that our combined efforts had yielded something. From my perspective, there was also a sense of relief that I hadn't made a complete fool of myself or suffered the humiliation of not winning the requisite 5% of the vote, without which the party would have forfeited the £500 deposit they had paid on my behalf. At least I could hold my head up high.

Although my agent, Sean Lever, sent a message of congratulations to all the Northamptonshire candidates, I was surprised that party HQ had not thought to arrange for some sort of generic message of gratitude to be circulated on behalf of Nigel and/or Richard. I was impervious to any slight, but I do know that it was disappointing to some of the candidates who had worked even harder and, in most cases, for much longer than I had been able to do. Like me, they worked on their own time and expense, and for several of my colleagues, it felt ungracious and left a bad taste in the mouth. Although the party "only" won five seats (a stunning effort in itself), we had all contributed collectively to the even more magnificent 4 million-plus votes, and it would have been an appropriate gesture. Maybe they did, and it was just another glitch in communication in which my name was once again omitted...?

Predictably, and perhaps for the same reason, we weren't invited to the celebration party in London later that day. I only heard about it from my nephew, who was there to report on the event for the media. A charitable view might have been that the powers that be assumed most of us had had very long nights and therefore wouldn't have had much of an appetite for it. But in the light of subsequent remarks about the unsuitability of candidates, it seemed unlikely they'd given a second thought to those of us who'd worked tirelessly on behalf of the party. It would have been appropriate if we'd been at least given the chance to share in celebrating the achievement that we had collectively been a part of.

However, by midday, as members of the party, all candidates did receive an email circular from Nigel-not to thank us but with an invitation to donate more funds to the party for the umpteenth time. I guessed that whoever pressed the send button was simply striking while the iron was hot, and perhaps this time the call for funds was to cover the cost of the celebrations we hadn't been included in. But on this occasion, I declined, secure in the knowledge that there would be several more "retail opportunities" to part with my money and celebrate again at my expense. Indeed, I didn't have to wait long before I was invited to pay to go to the annual conference in September and only a couple of months after that to attend the 'Christmas party' (aka major fundraising event) in December. No rest for the wicked, and certainly no sign whatsoever of thanks for any of the hardworking PCs!

The only hint of gratitude was via a round-robin email circulated by the Head of Operations almost three weeks later, which asked us all to continue to be the 'point person' for our respective constituencies and, more importantly, to give the party feedback on our experience. Hopefully, as the party replenishes its depleted coffers with much-needed and deserved funding, it will be able to afford an HR person who can give them some much-needed guidance on etiquette, decorum, and PR...

Worse was to come four months later, and along with many others, I was unimpressed when NF continued his habit of alienating and falling out with people. He subsequently described 95% of those who stood on behalf of the party as "paper candidates." After the effort and diligence that so many of us had put in, these dismissive and disparaging remarks were offensive, tactless, and untrue. They showed a lack of gratitude and appreciation for those who had not only dared to put their heads above the parapet but also used their own resources and dedicated a great many hours on behalf of the party. Without us, Reform UK would have got significantly fewer votes. To infer that the votes that were won were solely because of the party itself or Farage and none by individual candidates was ill-informed and arrogant. It might have been true in a very few cases, but the remarks didn't reflect well on him.

A prerequisite for anyone aspiring to be an MP is a thick skin, and I am definitely equipped with that. However, a lot of those who stood as candidates had devoted a great deal of time and energy to the party. They found his comments unnecessary and were dismayed to have heard them from our leader, who did not endear himself to them. Similarly, when former co-deputy leader Ben Habib was later rewarded by being gradually frozen out of the party machine and, in a deliberate and calculated way, unceremoniously ousted from his position, subsequent remarks he made about his former ally were characteristically unnecessary and unedifying.

In the immediate aftermath of the election, the party membership hit 63,000, and the momentum continued to build in the months that followed. By the time of writing, nine months later, it had ballooned to more than 230,000- a figure which comprehensively outstripped that of the beleaguered Tory party, although over Christmas, the claims were publicly questioned by new Tory leader Kemi Badenoch.[39]

The newly elected Reform UK MPs talked publicly about getting "Nigel into No.10," and there was a strong expectation that the party could win between 50 and 100 seats at the next General Election. This was partly due to the hope that the "red wall" seats, which Boris Johnson had "borrowed" from the traditional Labour heartlands in 2019, could be annexed by Reform in 2029 as Keir Starmer and his likely successors struggle in power, while the rudderless Conservatives continue to implode.

***

Long seen as a right-wing irritant, Labour should ignore Reform UK at their peril, as Farage is now gunning for and

---

[39] *Vicki Roskams, a PC who came second in the North Wales seat of Alyn and Deeside for Reform was suspended from the party for suggesting that new Conservative leader Kemi Badenoch was right to question whether Reform membership had reached 140,000 members in December 2024, claiming that the figure included a dog called Maverick who was listed as a "young member". The party denied this and invited the media to inspect their IT systems and corroborate the numbers.*

destabilising the Labour heartland. In a TV interview, he set his sights on being a thorn in their side after the election, promising to "change politics forever."

In his first press conference as an MP, he said: "The political establishment is in fear in private as to what happened last night with those results in the election."

When he returned to frontline politics and took over as head of the party in June, he said that he wanted "first to get millions of votes" and "second, to establish a bridgehead in parliament." He had achieved both aims. He promised to use his platform in Parliament to achieve his long-time goal of scrapping the First Past the Post electoral system, highlighting the party's 14% vote share, which had yielded just five MPs.

"Above all, what we're going to do from today is we're going to professionalise the party, we're going to democratise the party, and those few bad apples that have crept in will be long gone, and we will never have any of their type back in our organisation."

He denied that he would join any pact with the Tories, saying he would prefer to "let the Conservative Party tear themselves apart," and added, "We're going to focus on going after the Labour vote instead."

Keir Starmer will go down in the history books as having led Labour to a landslide victory in the 2024 general election, but with the smallest share of the electoral vote of any majority government since record-keeping of the popular vote began in 1830. His victory was a loveless one, simply the result of a marginal swing in an anti-Tory election in which the electorate voted against them for their failure to deliver over the last fourteen years. This was emphasised by his approval ratings after 100 days in office, which had fallen at a faster rate than any previous PM excluding the humiliation that Liz Truss put the Conservative Party through in only managing to survive 49 days in no.10.

As the Conservative party moved 'faster towards disaster', many voters had asked themselves how much worse it could actually be under Labour, but they would soon have their answer. Sir "Fear" himself got fewer votes than Jeremy Corbyn and only 34% of the vote. But because of FPTP, Labour secured two-thirds of the seats. However, they only increased their share of the vote by 1.06%, yet still ended up with a 200-seat majority, although their vote was less than the Corbyn campaign in 2017. Something other than First Past the Post is needed because, as it stands, the current government doesn't have a mandate. With only 33.8% of the vote, this means that 66.2% of votes were against them. It looks even worse when you take into consideration the low turnout of only 60% of all people eligible to vote. This shows that Labour got 34% of 60%, which represents just 20% of the entire voting population. This means that 80% did not vote for them, which strengthens the very strong argument for electoral reform.

6th July

After the first proper night's sleep that I'd had for many weeks, I woke with mixed feelings of both disappointment and relief that I hadn't won the seat, although I had known from the outset that it was highly unlikely. However, with each day of my campaign lost through not being allowed to get started, I was hostage to the science of diminishing returns.

I was confident that I hadn't simply taken votes in my constituency away from the Tories, as Mr Hollobone had inferred in the unnecessarily unpleasant exchange of words at the conference centre on election night (NB: a poll later found that most Reform voters would not have voted Conservative even without Farage's party). But I also knew that I had taken votes from Labour too. Between us all, Reform had given both the main parties a lot to think about. At the end of the day, Labour didn't win a mandate, and the Tories were now toast and beyond salvage.

In reality, and despite great encouragement to the contrary from masses of supporters, I knew that I wasn't in too much danger of being elected. On top of which, I recognised that I was too old to be a first-time MP. Although I seemed to have gained traction with a wide demographic of voters, my experiences confirmed my views that the ideal age for a first-time MP is someone in their late 30s or early 40s, with a blend of age, real-life experience, commercial expertise, and energy. That said, by winning their seats, Nigel, Richard Tice, and Rupert Lowe all contradicted my theory, as they were all 60 years old or more. However, both Nigel and Rupert had already been politicians in the European government, and Richard and Rupert had both been very successful in their respective business careers.

Conversely, some of the first-time, twenty-something-year-old MPs, if not actually adolescents, displayed similar traits, combined with a lack of life experience-the latter surely being a fundamental requisite for holding a position of such importance. Although our democracy allows anyone (unless specifically barred due to criminal convictions, etc.) the chance to be elected as an MP and represent a constituency, I have always felt that there should be a minimum age limit of at least 30, or preferably older, combined with a requirement to have been a taxpayer for, say, 8 years. This would lend credence to the idea that candidates had a combination of life experience and suitable business credentials. However, I'm aware that this would be deemed both ageist and elitist, neither of which would be approved of in the 'modern' (woke) society in which we exist. But as previously noted, I think it's of great concern that so many Labour MPs, and especially members of the cabinet, are so-called 'career politicians,' which strikes me as a euphemism for never having actually had a career outside the public sector or the trade unions.

Reform UK was woefully disorganised, shambolic, and unprofessional at times, but they acknowledged their many shortcomings. Given more time, better organisation, and greater resources, the result could have been even better. By the time of the next general election, under party chairman Zia Yusuf, it will be as he has already helped the party grow from zero official constituency branches to more than 400 and this is part of what it desperately needs to be properly structured and democratised. It also needs checks and balances. To this end, a new constitution was announced ahead of the (September 2024) autumn party conference, where members were assured that it would be transformed from a limited company, in which Farage held a minority stake, into one which gave them more control than him. However, his bombastic leadership style is such that, despite this, he appears to have remained in complete control and seems to change policies without reference to anyone else. An effective governance system, one that doesn't just go through one person, needs to be imposed and adhered to.

The party has gained huge momentum throughout and since the 2024 General Election campaign and now has a very clear identity. The nightmare scenario for the mainstream parties is that Reform gets its act together before the next election. Its ascendancy has been astonishing, but it needs to maintain the inexorable momentum. Like all political parties, it must broaden its appeal to the young and apathetic, especially via social media. If the party can secure a substantial amount of funding, then it will be able to run a much more targeted campaign based on the sort of data it doesn't currently have. It will also be able to employ full-time staff and build an efficient nationwide party machine with local activists and councillors.

In the meantime, attracting voters with soundbite politics may be easy in the short term, but the policies listed in the party "contract" now need properly structured forensic detail, without which they are in danger of slipping up. The party is likely to succeed in its quest to become the government's official opposition but it's easy to 'throw rocks' from the sidelines and be reactive from that position and if it wins the next general election they will need to be more proactive.

Despite lacking the depth of talent in the party, Reform UK has come of age. It is no longer a 'one-trick pony,' a protest party, or a one-man band. Now that Reform, as the "party of common sense," represents a distinctly more credible challenge to the two-party duopoly, it can't afford for any one person to be bigger than the party, as is currently the case.

I'm not sure I would describe my truncated campaign as fun with a capital 'F' during the intensive time that I was actually embroiled in it. I certainly learned a huge amount (enough for another book!), but as the press officer had cautioned it would be, it had been a rollercoaster ride, which was certainly exhilarating at times. In retrospect, once the dust had settled, I can say that it was a challenging and rewarding experience, most of which took place over the agonisingly short timescale of less than four weeks.

In motor racing, coming second is often referred to as being first of the losers and I hadn't even managed to do that, although I still made the podium by coming third in the rankings. More seriously, I was very proud to have played a small part in a political revolution and the start of a 'Turquoise Tidal Wave,' which I believe represents new hope for the future. I am convinced it will provide credible and much-needed opposition to the future Labour government, and ultimately, a viable alternative. I had done what I set out to do-namely, providing people in Kettering with a credible alternative to vote for, with my name to put a cross against in the polling booths. Although I didn't have a realistic chance of winning the seat, I amassed 8,468 votes (16.9%) from a standing start. In doing so, I took some away from the two main parties, especially giving the Conservatives a bloody nose. Thus, I achieved at least part of my aim, while contributing to the energy, optimism, and momentum of Reform UK.

Whether they were voting for Farage, the party, or just me, Crispian Besley, we all knew the combination was highly unlikely to win the seat that I contested. However, we could all at least take some satisfaction in having made a sizeable dent in both the main parties' counts in Kettering. There was still a sense of "could have/should have done better," in that I had only scratched the surface. Undoubtedly, I would have done better if only I'd had the benefit of the full six weeks-or even just four-in which to campaign. That additional time would also have allowed me to enlist help in embracing social media to a far greater extent than I was able to.

Apart from not beating Hollobone into an even more pleasing and satisfying second place, my biggest regret was not doing even better for each and every one of the 8,468 people who were brave enough to put their faith and trust in someone they had never met until only a few short weeks before the general election. Their support was genuinely humbling, as was the tireless efforts and support of those who selflessly volunteered to help me so much. Not being able to repay them for their loyalty to a greater extent did not sit easily with me, so this book, which incidentally took me a lot longer to write than I had time available to campaign, is for each and every one of them!

Epilogue

Despite having written a book on a completely different and unrelated subject about crime in motorsport it hadn't crossed my mind to put pen to paper on this topic until one of my many lifelong Conservative-voting friends patiently listened to me relating some of my experiences and anecdotes. He found them sufficiently interesting to suggest that they'd make a good subject for an article in a journal such as *The Spectator*, and that was the catalyst for what followed.

When I suggested to my agent, Sean Lever that I was considering putting my thoughts and anecdotes down in writing and structuring this book in diary form, he was incredibly supportive and agreed that my experience could benefit others who might consider putting themselves forward as PPCs in the future. He also understood that reminding existing and potential members, along with others, of the incredible result that Reform UK achieved against all odds-despite a lack of resources-might also benefit the party by highlighting its ongoing need for funding and anyway everyone loves an underdog.

He helpfully suggested that I inform Reform's Press and PR contacts about my project, and as I offered to donate a percentage of any royalties to the party, I expected an enthusiastic response. However, I didn't receive a reply for weeks. The project was simply referred to the party's lawyers, who reminded me that I had signed an NDA (Non-Disclosure Agreement) which forbade me from divulging "trade secrets," although, if any existed, I wasn't privy to them anyway. By the time the party secretary and lawyer had approved the manuscript, the IT factotum (who had presumably gone back to his day job after, like me, failing to win the seat he contested) had barred me from accessing the Kettering email address, which I had been asked and agreed to caretake and keep an eye on and act as the point person for. I was also removed from any internal news releases and all WhatsApp groups, without reference or notification. Given that I had put considerable effort into promoting the party and gaining a respectable amount of votes, I found this petty, discourteous and shortsighted.

Meanwhile, I received several communications from the party asking me to consider standing as a candidate in the local council elections from enthusiastic young volunteers who had no record of and were oblivious to my existing involvement or the fact that I had already stood as a PPC in the 2024 General Election. This suggests that Reform UK still needs to join up the dots and is seriously uncoordinated in its approach and organisation so it has a long way to go when it comes to professionalising its operations. If it is to continue building on its success and become the official opposition in time for the next general election, Reform UK must improve. After all, the country is in desperate need of REFORM!

GLOSSARY

BBC British Broadcasting Corporation

BoE Bank of England

BMA British Medical Association

BNP British National Party

CBI Confederation of British Industry

DNO Delegated Nominating Officer

DVLA Driver and Vehicle Licensing Agency

DWP Department for Work and Pensions

ECHR European Court of Human Rights

EU European Union

GDP Gross Domestic Product

GDPR General Data Protection Regulation

GE General Election

GLC Greater London Council

FPTP First Past the Post

HBOS Halifax Bank of Scotland

HS2 High Speed Two

HQ Headquarters

IFS Institute of Fiscal Studies

IMF The International Monetary Fund

IPSA Independent Parliamentary Standards Association

IT Information Technology

LSE London School of Economics

MEP Member of the European Parliament

MP Member of Parliament

MoT Ministry of Transport

NATO North Atlantic Treaty Alliance

NDA Non Disclosure Agreement

NEC National Exhibition Centre

NHS National Health Service

OBR Office for Budget Responsibility

OECD Organisation for Economic Co-operation and Development

OFCOM Office of Communication

ONS Office for National Statistics

PC Parliamentary Candidate

PM Prime Minister

PPC Prospective Parliamentary Candidate

PPS Parliamentary Private Secretary

QE Quantitive Easing

SDP Social Democratic Party

SME Small, Medium Size Enterprise

SNP Scottish National Party

SMTC St Moritz Toboggan Club

SUV Sports Utility Vehicle

UKIP United Kingdom Independence Party

UKPGE UK Parliamentary General Election

VAT Value added tax

WHO World Health Organisation

INDEX

Printed in Dunstable, United Kingdom

64705009R00178